The God Who Prays

The God Who Prays

A Forty-Day Meditation on Jesus' Farewell Prayers

John 16:23–18:1; Matthew 26:36–54; 27:45–46; Luke 23:34

Douglas D. Webster

CASCADE *Books* • Eugene, Oregon

THE GOD WHO PRAYS
A Forty-Day Meditation on Jesus' Farewell Prayers

Cascade Books
An Imprint of Wipf and Stock Publishers
199 W. 8th Ave., Suite 3
Eugene, OR 97401

www.wipfandstock.com

PAPERBACK ISBN: 978-1-4982-9376-1
HARDCOVER ISBN: 978-1-4982-9378-5
EBOOK ISBN: 978-1-4982-9377-8

Cataloguing-in-Publication data:

Webster, Douglas D.

The God who prays : a forty-day meditation on Jesus' farewell prayers / Douglas D. Webster.

Eugene, OR: Cascade Books, 2017 | Includes bibliographical references.

Identifiers: ISBN 978-1-4982-9376-1 (paperback) | ISBN 978-1-4982-9378-5 (hardcover) | ISBN 978-1-4982-9377-8 (ebook)

1. Bible. N.T. John 16–17. 2. Prayer. I. Title.

BS2615.2 W43 2017 (print) | BS2615.2 (ebook)

Manufactured in the U.S.A.   01/16/17

Claudette Penôt-Chan

"You prepare a table before me"

Contents

CONTENTS

A Learning Curve

Picture yourself with the disciples in the upper room. Given all the experiences described in the Gospels from the wedding feast in Cana of Galilee to the triumphal entry into Jerusalem this is the experience that stirs my imagination the most. *The God Who Prays* is our third and final meditative journey into Jesus' discipleship sermon. This study follows *The God Who Kneels* (John 13) and *The God Who Comforts* (John 14–16:22). We have imagined ourselves at the table with Jesus, feet clean and souls humbled. We ate the bread and drank from the cup. We sang a hymn and walked with Jesus through the streets of Jerusalem. We crossed the Kidron Valley and climbed the hill to the garden of Gethsemane. We have paid close attention to Jesus' teaching and asked the same questions the disciples did. We prayed our way into the upper room so we could enter into the discipleship experience. If you're like me, you are a little disappointed for having waited so many years to give Jesus' upper room discourse the kind of attention it deserves.

There is an escalating challenge in Jesus' discipleship sermon. Each successive phase requires us to think deeper and pray harder. Children can understand and confess Jesus Christ as Lord, but in the upper room discipleship is an adult challenge. In *The God Who Kneels* we focused on the sacrificial continuum from foot-washing to cross-bearing. John 13 begins with two simple object lessons, the towel and basin, the bread and cup. We focused on the close relationship between the divine atonement and the practice of discipleship and discovered that the trajectory from menial foot-washing to the atonement is intentional. Jesus began with an object lesson so physical and visual that it embodied the meaning and the mission of the gospel. "I have set you an example that you should do as I have done for you."

We can identify with Jesus on bended knee more readily than we can follow his reasons for an untroubled heart or enter into his prayer of consecration. This may be why some believers assume that the upper room discourse only consists of Jesus' foot-washing and his immediate commentary on love. We can grasp the object lesson, but we struggle to comprehend the comfort Jesus sought to give us. The learning curve is steep. Jesus expects us to grasp the deep comfort that comes by faith in Christ's second coming, the *Parousia,* and in the gift of the Holy Spirit, the *Paraclete,* and in the *Passion* of Christ's life, death, and resurrection, and in Christ's abiding *Presence.* Like the disciples, we are hardly in the mood to hear about the world's hate, but Jesus insists on preparing us for the world's animosity. In *The God Who Comforts,* the second phase of Jesus's discipleship sermon, we are challenged to follow Christ into the real hope rooted in the Word and Spirit of God.

The weariness of the disciples didn't stop Jesus from going deeper. He felt the pressure of it being their last night together before the crucifixion. His aim was to prepare the disciples for what was about to take place, Judas's betrayal, Peter's denial, the disciples' abandonment, and his condemnation by the religious and political authorities. But beyond that he wanted to reassure the disciples of their everlasting life and enduring hope. Late at night, on the streets of Jerusalem, Jesus never stopped encouraging and comforting the disciples. "I have much more to say to you," Jesus said, "more than you can now bear." But he pressed on knowing that the Spirit of truth would guide them *and us* into all the truth (John 16:13). In *The God Who Prays,* the third and final phase of Jesus' discipleship sermon, we move into Jesus' spiritual direction on prayer (16:23-33) and meditate on his prayer of consecration (John 17:1-26). Feeding daily on the word of Christ strengthens the disciples' hearts and minds. I came to see these daily meditations as mana-in-the-morning devotionals. They were usually written between 5-8 a.m. That's when my mind and heart seem best for meditating on Scripture. These daily meditations are probably not for the person who wants a quick heartwarming thought for the day. They require the reader to think deeply and prayerfully about the Word of God.

DAY I

A New Way of Asking

"In that day you will no longer ask me anything."
John 16:23.

We can hardly reconcile Jesus' promise, "In that day," with the typical behavior of today's believer. Many of us are like the disciples still struggling in the pre-passion mode. We want to be around Jesus, but we don't quite understand who he is or what he wants us to do. Our questions expose our unbelief. Our concerns betray weak faith. We sound like Philip when he said to Jesus, "Show us the Father and that will be enough for us," or like doubting Thomas when he laid down his ultimatum, "Unless I see the nail marks in his hands. . . . I will not believe." We can be all about Jesus but miss out what it means to follow him. We can insist on answers that Jesus never gave or a confirmation that Jesus never promised.

Our risen and ascended Lord expects his Spirit-gifted followers to ask different questions and request different things than what the early disciples were concerned about before Christ's resurrection and the gift of the Holy Spirit. The confusion and doubt that characterized the disciples' daily interaction with Jesus during his earthly ministry was meant to undergo a dramatic shift. The typical inquisitive dialogue that Jesus had with his followers is about to change from doubt to devotion. Instead of asking Jesus to explain himself, his followers will be expected to intercede on behalf of others, praying in his name. They will sound a lot more like Jesus than their old willful, doubting, agitated, hesitant selves.

Jesus promised a dramatic shift in confidence. The long debate in the mind of the disciples over Jesus' identity was to come to an end. Instead of confusion, conviction; instead of perplexity, passion. The bold prayer in Jesus' name replaces the gnawing question, "Is Jesus the one? Is Jesus the Son of God?"

Jesus promises the disciples a transition from pre-passion inquisitiveness to post-passion boldness. A good marriage may serve as a helpful analogy for the transition Jesus promises. As a couple considers their commitment to one another there is a period of indecision and questioning. A man and a woman may fall head over heels in love, but wisdom calls for a process of discernment. It is one thing to be infatuated with being in love, it is another to thing to be in love with the beloved. Genuine love calls for serious soul-searching, at the end of which a turning point is reached. The couple moves from debate and doubt and to determination and decision. "Yes, this is the one." They exchange their holy marriage vows, pledging themselves and all they are and will be to each other in an exclusive, permanent, and holy covenantal relationship. The marriage rightly determines a whole new set of questions. Instead of debating and doubting the suitability of the other person in the relationship, husband and wife enter into life together with a joyful and trusting confidence in each other and in their shared purpose.

Jesus' promise was meant to reassure the disciple, especially the inquisitive, artistic and sensitive disciple, who feels that even the most basic question of Jesus' identity must remain open and unresolved. Such a person is inclined to think that doubt is always more honest than devotion. Yet Jesus promises relief to the doubting disciple who feels that a courageous and confident faith depends on their own discernment and determination. It doesn't. Like everything else, it depends on Jesus and his finished work, the work he was sent by the Father to do. The "self" was never meant to be the arbitrator of a confident and resilient faith. If the transition from inquiry and training to conviction and mission is left to us we will always find doubts and distractions that lead us back into uncertainty and confusion.

There comes a time when we need to let go and move on from our old inquiries, doubts, and hesitancies. Like the disciples we need to shift out of training mode and move into mission. The power to do this does not lie in ourselves, in our willpower, but in God's will and power. Humanly speaking we shall never get to the bottom of our frailty and doubt. We can only rise above them by the power of the resurrection and the gift of Christ's abiding presence. The shift from doubt to dedication is the fulfillment of a promise, but we should be clear on Jesus' expectation.

Reflections on the Way

How do you understand the difference between pre-passion inquisitiveness and post-passion boldness?

What helps believers move from doubt to devotion?

How do we shift from training mode to mission?

Compare Jesus' expectations for post-Resurrection maturity with your own expectations.

DAY 2

The Jesus Prayer

"Very truly I tell you, my Father will give you
whatever you ask in my name. Until now you
have not asked for anything in my name."
John 16:23-24

The move from inquiry to intimacy and from doubt to devotion is reflected here in prayer. The disciples' daily dialogue with God replaces the questions and doubts that characterize a pre-passion state of limbo. Jesus marks the transition from confusion to confession with an exclamation, "Very truly I tell you," an endorsement, "my Father," and an empowerment, "in my name." Prayer's promised efficaciousness, "whatever you ask," is locked in to our relationship with the triune God. The Father is the source of every good and perfect gift. The Son, in whose name we pray, gives the purpose and the passion for "whatever" we ask. And our Advocate, the Holy Spirit, guides us into all truth. Prayer as conversation with God is not controlled by anything other than the will of the Father, the glory of the Son, and the wisdom of the Spirit. Any thought that Jesus writes a blank check to be filled in by our hopes and dreams misses the point not only of prayer but of our intimacy with God.

We tend to read "whatever you ask" without hearing Jesus frame our prayer in the will of the Father and in the name of the Son. "Whatever" seems broadly inclusive of anything we want it to be. But we don't want to forget the strategic transition in the life of the disciple from self-rule to Christ's rule. The two qualifying phrases, "in that day," and "until now" signals an eschatological break from pre-passion inquisitiveness to post-passion boldness. Our *asking* undergoes a remarkable change, because our requests are vetted by the Father, Son, and Holy Spirit. Now even the most *spiritual* and *well-intentioned* prayers are subject to the kind of scrutiny consistent with divine intimacy. When the "whatever" reflects a true oneness with God our prayers will be more radical and less predictable. Jesus frames this "whatever" in a very distinctive way.

Consider an urgent prayer request, to pray for a definitive end to Ebola in West Africa. This call for prayer went out in the Spring of 2015. Although the disease has been largely contained through the valiant and sacrificial efforts of medical teams, new cases continued to be reported in Guinea and Sierra Leone. Ebola had a devastating impact on public health throughout West Africa, causing a serious setback in the fight against malaria. People suffering from malaria and other health concerns were afraid to go to clinics for fear of being quarantined for Ebola. The request to pray for the end of Ebola came from the director of a medical team hoping to go to Ghana in the Fall of 2015. The previous year's medical mission trip to northern Ghana had been cancelled due to the Ebola outbreak and now the team faced the same sad prospect unless there was a definitive end to Ebola. The Ghanian and western leaders set a deadline of August 1, 2015, praying that there would be zero cases of Ebola in West Africa. "We have not given up hope," wrote the director, "but recognize that we need God to work mightily to finish this outbreak."

The church throughout West Africa and believers around the world had been praying earnestly for more than a year for a definitive end to the devastating Ebola outbreak. Could there be any more spiritually authentic and compassionate request to make in Christ's name? Surely not. To pray for the health safety of medical teams and the hundreds if not thousands of patients who gather for treatment makes perfect sense. Nevertheless to pray for the definitive end to a devastating disease by a set date so plans can proceed for the mission trip faces a radical new kind of scrutiny.

The promise, "my Father will give you whatever you ask in my name," is made by the one who prayed, "Father, if you are willing, take this cup from me; yet not my will, but yours be done" (Luke 22:42). Since the "whatever" is controlled by the will of the Father and is in the name of the Son, the possibility of sacrificial service marked by the cross remains the answer we may not like to hear. We may need to pray for wisdom to proceed with a modified medical operation to reduce risk and focus on acute care. We may need to pray for courage for a select group of medical personnel willing to risk the dangers of a lingering deadly disease. To pray this way is difficult because there is no end to the definitive dangers facing Christians who carry out the will of God.

Jesus concludes this section on prayer by saying to his disciples, "I have told you these things, so that in me you may have peace. In this world you will have trouble. But take heart! I have overcome the world" (John 16:33). We note the juxtaposition of his peace and the world's trouble. The promise of answered prayer is in keeping with the fact that "in this world you will have trouble." Whatever we ask for in his name will not be trouble free. God's rich blessings and the world's deep troubles persist until Jesus Christ ends all evil in the final judgment. Until that day we take up our cross daily and follow Jesus with the assurance that whatever we ask in the name of the Son, through the wisdom of the Spirit, the Father will grant.

Praying in the name of Jesus is made possible by the completed work of Christ's passion. Until now the disciples have not really understood that Jesus is God, that the Father and the Son are one, and that they are equally God. This will all change when the Son glorifies the Father "by finishing the work" the Father gave him to do (John 17:4). Praying in the name of Jesus does not mean adding a specific tag line, "in Jesus' name," but it does mean praying in such a way that "the Father may be glorified in the Son" (John 14:13). The Jesus prayer means that we are making our real home in Christ and living our lives in obedience to all that Jesus taught (John 15:7). When these conditions are satisfied, "our wills our identified with the will of God; we are then praying for what

He desires to give and waits to give until we recognize Him as its source so that our reception of it will strengthen our faith and not encourage our neglect of Him." William Temple continues, "This means that the essential act of prayer is not the bending of God's will to ours—of course not—but the bending of our wills to His."[1]

Reflections on the Way

What should we expect when we pray in the name of the one who was crucified?

How do disciples and pagans pray differently?

How does prayer deepen our dependence upon the Lord?

As you reflect on Jesus' words, what should you pray for?

1. Temple, *Readings in St. John's Gospel*, 305.

DAY 3

Asking for Joy

"Ask and you will receive, and your
joy will be complete."
John 16:24

Joy—complete joy—is the byproduct of the Jesus prayer. God's
answer to our prayers is calculated to bring joy—real joy, lasting
joy, the kind of joy the world cannot take away. We start out in
life asking anyone who will listen for everything that will make us
happy. We end up in the Christian life asking God for everything
that will glorify him. Prayer qualifies as one of the ultimate tests
of maturity. From a very young age we learn how to ask. We learn
how to ask, beg, whine, and demand what we want. If you don't
believe me, but I know you do, just hang around a toddler for an
afternoon! Some people never outgrow the toddler stage. They
keep on asking, begging, whining, manipulating, and demanding
to have their own way. We all have been infected by the survival of
the fittest mentality. Most of us are pretty devious and persistent
at getting our way. The pursuit of happiness, especially of *my* happiness, is deeply rooted in our souls. We are like King David with
Bathsheba, when he saw what he wanted, he took what he saw.

Jesus began the Sermon on the Mount by talking about
"happiness" and ends his last discipleship sermon by talking
about complete joy. Yet if we're honest, we have to acknowledge
that Jesus' understanding of happiness is about as different from
the American pursuit of happiness as you can imagine. We may
use "happiness" and "joy" interchangeably, but Jesus gave a very

distinct meaning to being happy, one that the world cannot fathom. America's "Beatitudes" run something like this: "Blessed are those who believe in themselves, for they will be successful." Or, "Blessed are those who are in touch with their feelings and free of any self-imposed guilt." Or again, "Blessed are those who are in good shape for they will be envied." Jesus' alternative route to happiness begins with a declaration of utter dependence on the mercy of God. To be truly blessed is to become by the grace of God so self-aware of our sinfulness and brokenness that we turn to God for salvation. Worldly happiness and Jesus' joy are radically different from each other. If we do not grasp this truth we will never experience the promise of answered prayer leading to complete joy. Disney's motto, "The Happiest Place on Earth," works for a theme park, but it doesn't work for the real world.

The movement from pre-passion inquisitiveness and doubt to post-passion devotion and discipleship involves a fundamental change in the believer's emotional outlook on life. The answers to prayer come not only in the form of truer worship, bolder witness, and a richer life together, they also come in the form of a deeper, more resilient joy.

In his book, *The First American Evangelical: A Short Life of Cotton Mather,* historian Rick Kennedy draws out the distinctive meaning of this satisfying joy. Cotton Mather (1663–1728) was a highly influential pastor and scholar whose vibrant evangelical faith in Christ coupled with an unshakeable confidence in the Bible as the Word of God inspired many New Englanders to remain faithful to Christ. At the age of eighteen, a few months before he graduated from Harvard with his master's degree, Cotton describes in his *Diary* his "closure with the Lord Jesus Christ," as a "glorious transaction" in which he affirmed "a covenant of redemption" with God.[1]

This "closure" became especially evident in how Cotton faced suffering and disappointment. He lost thirteen of his fifteen children. His first wife, Abigail, died as a result of a miscarriage when he was thirty-nine. He had spent days and nights by her bedside

1. Kennedy, *The First American Evangelical*, 30.

praying for her healing and felt "the blessed breezes of a particular faith" assuring him that Abigail would live.[2] When she died, "he noted the sting of 'a miscarriage of a particular faith.'"[3] He explained to his children, "It may be that the Lord will ere long enable me to penetrate further into the nature, meaning, and mystery of a particular faith; however, I have met with enough to awaken in me a more exquisite caution."[4] Cotton lived with a strong sense of human ignorance and fallibility and an even stronger sense of God's perfect sovereignty. He affirmed wholeheartedly what the Westminster Confession declared that the chief end of man was to glorify God and enjoy him forever. As Kennedy writes, "Cotton was humble. God was God. God was good. Cotton's job was to trust and obey. . . .[He] emphasized the glorifying and enjoying. He found divine sovereignty comforting. The doctrine encouraged joy in all situations."[5] A devastating measles outbreak in 1713 claimed the life of his second wife and his two newborn twins, but even that did not stop Cotton from asking "for the grace to be a model to his congregation, holy in conversation with people and disposed to enquire into the glory of his Savior."[6] Cotton Mather could have said with Job, "My joy in unrelenting pain—that I had not denied the words of the Holy One" (Job 6:10). At the age of fifty Cotton noted in his *Diary*, "My life is almost a continual conversation with Heaven."[7]

For a birthday surprise my son had a stack of my old family movies digitalized. These old 16 mm clips were shot on our cross-country road trips when my brother and I were ten to fifteen years old. They show us jumping into motel pools, playing baseball, celebrating birthdays, all the usual things that prompted parents in the 1960s to pull out the movie camera. But what struck both my wife and I was how happy my mother was. She seemed so

2. Ibid., 97.
3. Ibid.
4. Ibid.
5. Ibid., 96-97.
6. Ibid., 129.
7. Ibid.

carefree, always smiling, waving happily to the camera in almost every scene. We were the picture of a young, happy, healthy, loving family. But the death of my father from cancer at the age of forty-eight changed our lives. His dying plus my cancer put a tremendous strain on my mother. She became the principal caregiver for her in-laws, caring for my grandparents and my aunt through the extended ordeal of hospitals, insurance negotiations, dying, and funerals. I'd say my mother's life became very hard emotionally and economically, but she never wavered in her devotion to Christ and in her care for her sons. The carefree young mother shown on our home movies became a resilient saint, free from any bitterness and complaint. She experienced deep suffering and disappointment, but my brother and I knew that she resonated with Nehemiah's one liner, "Do not grieve, for the joy of the Lord is your strength" (Neh 8:10).

Reflections on the Way

How resilient is your joy?

What can we take away from Cotton Mather's example of devotion and fortitude?

Have you ever shared Job's perspective, "My joy in unrelenting pain . . ."?

How can we encourage one another to know the joy of the Lord?

DAY 4

A New Conversation

"Though I have been speaking figuratively,
a time is coming when I will no longer use
this kind of language but will tell you plainly
about my Father." John 16:25

The disciples are about to hear Jesus' plainest speech yet about his Father when he offers his prayer of consecration (John 17:1-26). The explicit Christology of the canonical epistles begins here on the streets of Jerusalem as Jesus walks to Gethsemane. He will continue the conversation on the road to Emmaus following the resurrection when Jesus explains "what was said in all the Scriptures concerning himself" (Luke 24:27).

Remember Jesus' response to John the Baptist's question, "Are you the one who is to come, or should we expect someone else?" He said, "Go back and report to John what you hear and see. The blind receive sight, the lame walk, those who have leprosy are cleansed, the deaf hear, the dead are raised, and the good news is proclaimed to the poor. Blessed is anyone who does not stumble on account of me" (Matt 11:3-6). Jesus' response makes a clear allusion to messianic prophecy, but it lacked the explicit affirmation John undoubtedly sought. Why was Jesus reluctant to say boldly, "I am the Messiah!"?

Jesus' elusive response fits a pattern in which he avoided direct answers to questions about his authority. He was reluctant to publicize his work. When the Jewish religious leaders confronted him, demanding to know by what authority he taught and acted, he declined to comment (Luke 20:1-8). He repeatedly demanded secrecy from those he healed (Mark 1:44; 5:43; 7:36; 8:26), and he insisted on silence when the demon-possessed cried out that he was the Son of God (Mark 1:34; Luke 4:41). Even the disciples were warned not to tell anyone that he was the Christ (Matt 16:20) or to reveal their experience of Jesus' transfiguration (Matt 17:9).

Jesus intentionally used "figurative" language to convey his identity. His enigmatic and cryptic speech was necessary in order to redefine the meaning of the messiah. The people thought they needed a political savior to rescue them from Rome, but what they needed was a redemptive Savior to rescue them from sin and death. Not until the end did Jesus clearly and publicly admit he was the Messiah. When the high priest asked, "Are you the Christ, the Son of the Blessed One?" Jesus responded directly, "I am. . .And you will see the Son of Man sitting at the right hand of the Mighty One and coming in the clouds of heaven" (Mark 14:61-62). Pastor Helmut Thielicke observed, "It is striking that Jesus uses these predicates of majesty when he is being delivered up to death, exposed to humiliation, and plunged into the passion, so that the confession of his messiahship can no longer give a wrong impression of loftiness nor lead to a theology of glory, but engulfs us in the depths of his destiny."[1]

The conversation shifts from pre-passion "hiddenness" to post-passion explicitness. Like a vintage wine the truth of Christ required time to age. Jesus revealed his messianic self-identity by building on the Old Testament types. He is the ladder reaching to heaven (John 1:51) and the one lifted up just as Moses lifted up the snake in the wilderness (John 3:14). He is greater than Jacob because he provides living water (John 4:14). He is the true bread from heaven that gives life to the world (John 6:33). He is the good shepherd who lays down his life for the sheep (John 10:11). This is what he meant when he said that he had been speaking "figuratively." But following the resurrection the disciples were able to look back with the help of the Holy Spirit and understand in a fresh way what Jesus had been saying all along. This remarkable

1. Thielicke, *The Evangelical Faith*, 2:352.

paradigm shift gave the apostles a whole new way to see Christ in the Old Testament.

On a visit to South Africa biblical scholar Sidney Greidanus witnessed a perfect illustration of this paradigm shift. He was being driven to a man-made lake which supplies water to Cape Town. Along the way they passed through a scenic valley. Greidanus was impressed by the vivid shades of green covering the valley floor. To his surprise, on their return trip a half hour later the whole valley looked white, for it was covered with white flowers. "Astonished, I wondered why I had missed seeing these flowers on our way up. I turned around and amazingly saw mostly green scenery, just a hint of a flower here and there; I looked ahead and again was surprised to see the whole valley white with flowers. Why was it that the valley appeared green when we traveled west, and white when we traveled east? The valley, I learned, was covered with flowers that turn toward the sun. When we drove west into the sun we saw the green backside of the flowers, but when we reversed course and had the sun behind us, we saw the flowers pointing to the sun." Greidanus continues, "That is the way it was with Jesus' disciples.After Jesus' resurrection, when they read the Old Testament in the light of their crucified and risen Lord, the whole Old Testament lit up . . . [with] 'a thousand points of light' pointing to Jesus the Messiah."[2]

I communicate very differently with my grandchildren than I do with my adult children. Young children require more creativity to clarify the message. They need images and metaphors to explain very simple things. Life's truths about life and death, good and evil, sex and sacrament, are introduced to them gradually and with great care. Likewise, God's Word reveals a process of divine communication that moves from figurative speech to plain speech and from the implicit to the explicit.

2. Greidanus, *Preaching Christ from the Old Testament*, 184.

Reflections on the Way

Why was Jesus more implicit than explicit about his own identity?

How does Jesus' pre-passion "hiddenness" influence our evangelism today?

How does Jesus' post-passion "explicitness" impact how we read the Old Testament?

The Bible reflects great care in how the story of redemption is told. How can we do the same?

DAY 5

In My Name

"In that day you will ask in my name. I am not saying that I will ask the Father on your behalf. No, the Father himself loves you because you have loved me and have believed that I came from God." John 16:26-27

Jesus is our redemptive mediator, not a middleman. We don't need a lobbyist passing our prayers up to the Father, we need the Advocate interceding for us at the right hand of the Father (Rom 8:34; Heb 7:25; 1 John 2:1). Jesus makes the covenant of grace possible through his redemptive intervention. "For there is one God and one mediator between God and mankind, the man Christ Jesus, who gave himself a ransom for all people" (1 Tim 2:5-6). A middleman negotiates a deal between the supplier and the consumer and receives his cut, but Jesus "appeared once for all at the culmination of the ages to do away with sin by the sacrifice of himself" (Heb 9:26). In him, "we have a great high priest who has ascended into heaven, Jesus the Son of God. . . . Let us then approach the throne of grace with confidence, so that we may receive mercy and find grace to help us in our time of need" (Heb 4:14,16).

Martin Luther focuses on the great encouragement of the little phrase "in My name." Luther writes, "It is the foundation on which prayer must rest. These words give to prayer the good quality and dignity that makes it acceptable to God. They also free us from all severe trials and from useless worries regarding our worthiness, worries that hinder our praying and frighten us more than anything else. From these words we gather that we should not be concerned or worried about our own worthiness but should forget about both worthiness and unworthiness and base our prayer on Christ and pray in his His name. . . . It is as though He were saying: 'My dear friend, it does not matter in what condition you are. If you cannot pray on your own authority and in your name—as indeed you should not—then please pray in My name. If you are not worthy and holy enough, let Me be holy and worthy enough for you.'"[1]

We claim Christ's mercy, not because the Father is angry and stern and needs to be appeased. Our direct access to God is based on the Father's love. As the Apostle Paul said, "the Spirit you received brought about your adoption to sonship. And by him we cry, 'Abba, Father'" (Rom 8:15). Jesus didn't die "to change God into love; he died to tell us that God is love. He came, not because God so hated the world, but because he so loved the world."[2] Matthew Henry reminds us that "the Father's love and good-will appointed Christ to be the Mediator; so that we owe Christ's merit to God's mercy in giving him for us."[3]

This direct access to the Father means that we can pray in much the same way that Jesus prays. He assures us that we have his access to the triune God. In saying this here he invites us to model our prayer after his prayer of consecration. Once again Jesus underscores a remarkable transition from pre-passion religion to post-passion communion. We are empowered to pray independent of a priest's presence or a pastor's piety or a written liturgy. If all believers have equal "access to the Father by one Spirit" why have we come to believe that pastors pray better at the bedside of a sick person than a believing member of the patient's family? (Eph 2:18). Why is there so much deference paid to *the pastor* as if the burden of ministry rests on his or her shoulders alone?

The notion that there is a special class of spiritual people dies hard. People cling to the idea of the heroic pastor who rushes to

1. Quoted in Bruner, *John*, 955.
2. Barclay, *John*, vol. 2, 201.
3. Quoted in Bruner, *John*, 955.

the hospital to pray with them before their 6:30 a.m. appendectomy. For some reason, the thought persists that the pastor has a special anointing from God that makes his prayer more efficacious and more consoling than the prayer of a close brother or sister in Christ. Too many believers hold this superstitious notion over the heads of their pastors and too many pastors feed this notion: the notion that the church has not been supportive or represented unless the pastor prays by the bedside; the notion that the pastor's timely presence is as necessary as the medical doctor's. Hospital visitation is an important ministry for the entire congregation, including the pastor, and to do it well requires spiritual maturity, understanding, and compassion. Beseeching God for healing and for comfort is a necessary and vital ministry, but it is a ministry that belongs to the priesthood of all believers, and not exclusively, or even primarily, to the pastor.

Receive Jesus' bold pastoral statement as an encouragement: "I am not saying that I will ask the Father on your behalf." Jesus boldly rejects a false dependency based on a misperception of the Father's love. Look to Jesus for your salvation, but don't look to Jesus or anyone else to do your praying for you. Our mediator and intercessor, Jesus Christ, makes unlimited direct access possible for each and every disciple. Jesus will not be praying *for* us as much as he will be *with* us, because the Father sees in us, Christ himself, who is the object of our faith and love.[4] May we say with Cotton Mather, "My life is almost a continual conversation with Heaven."[5]

4. Brown, *John*, 735.

5. Kennedy, *The First American Evangelical*, 129.

Reflections on the Way

What does it mean for you that Jesus, the Mediator, removes the middleman between you and the Father?

How does praying in the name of Jesus take the pressure off of us?

Why do we attribute to pastors greater access to God?

How can prayer become for you a continual conversation with heaven?

DAY 6

Back to the Father

"I came from the Father and entered the world; now
I am leaving the world and going back to the Father."
John 16:28

With the cross only hours away Jesus was finished with his enigmatic and cryptic language. He was ready to speak plainly, and this is exactly what he does in his concise one-verse confession. We marvel that the most fundamental truth of the universe can be stated with such clarity and simplicity. Like the single melody line that the composer works into a full symphony these four phrases encompass the scope of Jesus' entire ministry. This single verse is a "brief summary of the whole historic work of Christ: clause answers clause: the Mission, the Nativity; the Passion, the Ascension."[1]

"I came from the Father." Our confession is based on Christ's confession. We are not original in our conviction. We believe in his testimony. There is no way of getting around this bold step of faith other than in believing that Jesus is in fact who he says he is. He is not a charismatic figure embellished by the Gospel writers or a great teacher whose sayings like Confucius's or Socrates's have contributed to his legend. No, he actually came from the Father. He is the incarnate one. "The Word became flesh and made his dwelling among us. We have seen his glory, the glory of the one and only Son, who came from the Father, full of grace and truth" (John 1:14). He is as the confession declares, "truly God and truly

1. Bruner, *John*, 956. Quoting Westcott.

Man . . .co-essential with the Father according to the Godhead . . . co-essential with us according to Manhood; like us in all things, sin apart . . ." The only way to know God is this way—his way! Jesus is not one option among many ways to God. He is the only way. The incarnate one transcended his transcendence: "Who, being in very nature God, did not consider equality with God something to be used to his own advantage; rather, he made himself nothing by taking the very nature of a servant, being made in human likeness" (Phil 2:6-7).

"I entered the world." Our conviction is this: the way to know God is to become like Jesus. Jesus is "the true light that gives light to everyone coming into the world. . . . He came to that which was his own, but his own did not receive him. Yet to all who did receive him, to those who believed in his name, he gave the right to become the children of God—children born not of natural descent, nor of human decision or a husband's will, but born of God" (John 1:9-13). Who we are and who we are becoming depends on the exemplary life of Jesus. Jesus shows us how God intended human life to be lived. Through his capacity to love, communicate, think, act, and worship, he demonstrated not only what it means to be spiritual but what it means to be human. His spirituality becomes the model for our worship. His teaching is the ground for our ethic; his self-understanding, the pattern for our self-awareness; his self-sacrifice, the paradigm of our service; his bodily resurrection, the hope of our resurrection. His method of evangelism becomes our strategy for witnessing, and his call for justice becomes our commitment.

"I am leaving the world." Our confidence is in the finished work of Jesus Christ. The mystery of the passion coheres with the mystery of the incarnation. "And being found in appearance as a man, he humbled himself by becoming obedient to death—even death on a cross!" (Phil 2:8). The same rationale behind God sending his Son is at work in the meaning of the cross. This is how God showed his love to us. "He sent his one and only Son into the world that we might live through him. This is love: not that we loved God, but that he loved us and sent his Son as atoning sacrifice for our sins" (1 John 4:9-10). Jesus' entire upper room discourse is framed by his realization that "the hour had come for him to leave this world and go to the Father. . . . Jesus knew that the Father had put all things under his power and that he had come from God and was returning to God. . ." (John 13:1, 3).

Our movies, art, literature, drama, poetry, and news media cover the horror of evil from virtually every angle, but provide little hope for redemption. The human story, even when it is told with pathos and creativity, continues to confirm that humanity cannot save itself. Everyone has a story but only one story redeems our story. The passion of Christ gathers up all of our sins and nature's evils—our idolatries, betrayals, addictions, deceptions, diseases, and hatreds, and nails them to the cross. The tragedy of evil and God's redemptive love leads slowly and painstakingly to the cross—all for the sake of our salvation. The necessity of this cruciform culmination was woven into the events of salvation history from the beginning.

"I am going back to the Father." Our consolation and hope is in our risen and ascended Lord. The crucified Messiah is the risen Lord. To divorce Jesus from the biblical testimony of the resurrection effectively annuls Christian faith and practice. If the bodily resurrection of Jesus did not take place, then the meaning of the incarnation, kingdom ethic, and atonement would have to be discounted. If the bones of Jesus disintegrated in a Palestinian tomb, then becoming like Jesus is a sad delusion. Without the bodily resurrection of Jesus, the Apostle Paul admitted that Christian preaching was useless, faith in Christ was futile, and the burden of sin remained. As far as Paul was concerned, Christianity without the resurrection had no credibility. If God did not raise Jesus from the dead, believers were false witnesses of God, without hope, who ought to be "pitied more than all people" (1 Cor 15:14-19). Without the resurrection the gospel not only doesn't make sense, it is in fact dishonest and deceptive. If there is no resurrection from the dead then death ends all and all are lost.

The necessity of the resurrection of Jesus was woven into the very nature of creation. If history's need points to the cross, creation's mysteries point to the resurrection. The meaning of the resurrection cannot be packaged into a neat foolproof apologetic, but it can be understood. We cannot explain it so as to control it or manipulate it, but we can marvel at its wisdom. We can grasp its meaning, comprehend its truth, but we cannot package it for easy consumption. From what we know of creation, the resurrection "makes sense." It fits. The resurrection was not some wild card, played at the end, which doesn't correspond with what we know of nature. The new biology fits in with the old biology. Like many things in science that we never would have expected to be true, the resurrection is consistent and coherent with what we know of reality. The same God who created the cosmos raised Christ from the dead. The more we know of this scientific world of ours, the greater the sheer wonder, astonishment, and amazement at the power of the resurrection. Wonder is not antithetical to understanding. Given what we know, not what we don't know, the resurrection makes perfect sense and evokes the truest amazement.

Jesus prefaced this concise summary of his mission by affirming his Father's love for his disciples, "because you have loved me and have believed that I came from God" (John 16:27). What the disciples believed mattered, not just to Jesus, but to the Father as well. Just as our belief in Christ's mission, incarnation, passion, and ascension, matters to the Father. Augustine believed that Jesus never left the Father and he never leaves the world.

> "In coming to the world He came forth in such a sense from the Father that He did not leave the Father behind; and that, on leaving the world, He goes to the Father in such a sense that He does not actually forsake the world. For He came forth from the Father because He is of the Father; and He came into the world, in showing to the world His bodily form, which He had received from the Virgin. He left the world by a bodily withdrawal, He proceeded to the Father by His ascension as man, but He forsook not the world in the ruling activity of His presence."[2]

2. Augustine, *Homilies on the Gospel of St. John*, 391.

Reflections on the Way

How do you grapple with the profound mystery that lies behind Jesus' simple phrases?

Why was it important for Jesus to return to the Father?

Do you believe that history points to the cross and creation points to the resurrection?

How can we grasp truths too great for humanistic consumption?

Well-Intentioned Disciples

"Then Jesus' disciples said, 'Now you are speaking clearly and without figures of speech. Now we
can see that you know all things and that you do
not even need to have anyone ask you questions.
This makes us believe that you came from God.'"

John 16:29-30

The disciples want to reassure Jesus that they understand. They
get it. They commend the clarity of his compact creed and
his straight-forward speech. They believe Jesus came from God.
Nicodemus made a similar claim at the outset of Jesus' ministry,
"Rabbi, we know that you are a teacher who has come from God"
(John 3:2). But the disciples' understanding of who Jesus is has
gone well beyond Nicodemus's compliment. Peter has already
made two strong confessions: "We have come to believe and to
know that you are the Holy One of God" (John 6:69), and "You
are the Messiah, the Son of the living God" (Matt 16:16). Even
so, some scholars debate the strength of the disciples' confession.
Jesus said that he "came forth" from the Father, which expresses his
union with the Father and the importance of his mission perhaps
more clearly than the disciple's statement that Jesus "came from"
God. Jesus claims that "he came *from the presence of God* and *out
of God*," whereas "the disciples confess no more than that He *came
from God*."[1]

1. Bruner, *John*, 956.

Yet the strength of the disciples' confession can be found in their reasoning, "Now we can see that you know all things and that you do not even need to have anyone ask you questions." They are indeed convinced that Jesus knows all things and that he even knows the questions on their minds before they ask him. Jesus is like the Father knowing what you need before you ask him (Matt 6:8). Their reasoning refers back to Jesus' prophecy, "In that day you will no longer ask me anything." The disciples are eager to re-assure Jesus that as far as they are concerned "that day" has already arrived. Jesus is answering their questions before they even have a chance to ask them. Coming at the end of Jesus' upper room discourse, this is a significant commendation. The disciples are tracking with Jesus. Their questions are being answered.

With that said, the disciples don't know what they don't know. Their desire to encourage Jesus by their response is well-intentioned, but naive. The pivotal transition from pre-passion naivete to post-passion mission has not yet happened. When Pentecost comes and the Holy Spirit has been given, then they will see the meaning of Jesus and his words in perspective. But for now they get the *confession* right and the *commitment* wrong. Getting the confession right is only half the battle. Like Peter at Caesarea Philippi when he made his bold confession, we may hear the Spirit but still end up in Satan's camp (Matt 16:23). Unless we see the true impact of our confession we will settle for a half-truth and when the crisis comes we will fall away.[2]

Well-meaning but misguided Christians have frequently cultivated a false enthusiasm based on a preconceived notion of Christ and the Christian life. They assume the validity of a certain understanding of Jesus Christ without testing their assumptions or scrutinizing their easily acquired convictions. An example of half-truth Christianity is Joel Osteen. His popularity leads many naive Christians into a popular folk religion that caters to the self. His fundamental message is a form of spirituality that you achieve for yourself. His famous tag line, "Your Best Life Now" celebrates personal success. Seated on the throne of his modern-ancient gospel

2. Newbigin, *The Light Has Come*, 221.

is the self. You are your own redemption. You decide whether you are going to mount up on eagles' wings and be successful. Osteen's Bible-less Jesus allows for a "flexodoxy" necessary to mass market salvation. His spirituality is therapeutic deism, seasoned with iconic references to the Bible and Jesus in the service of the American Dream. The power of positive thinking replaces prayers of confession. A material and emotional makeover is in lieu of Christian conversion. Feelings don't trump truth; feelings are the truth. You have to be true to your dreams if you are going to be true to yourself.

Jesus emphasized to his followers that a life of discipleship and costly commitment was the true follow-up to confession: "If anyone would come after me, he must deny himself and take up his cross and follow me" (Matt 16:24). Insight means actions, and action results in understanding. There is a lively exchange between confession and commitment that authenticates confession and purifies commitment. We cannot follow Jesus authentically any way we please. We must follow him according to his example through the power of the Holy Spirit. We do not naturally adopt a pattern of life that reflects Christ. We have too many preconceived notions of what life should be like to readily transform our thinking and change our actions according to the will of Christ. Sin is too deeply ingrained within and too manifest without for anyone to assume an automatic Christian maturity.

Secular people find it difficult to confess that Jesus is the Son of God, but Christians find it difficult to commit to costly discipleship. The language of losing one's life for Christ's sake sounds as mythical to many Christians as the virgin birth and the substitutionary atonement are to secular people. Yet precisely because Christians have been willing to risk their intellects in order to discover the truth revealed in Christ, they now must risk their lives in order to discover the fullness of life in Christ.

Reflections on the Way

What is the difference between a naive confidence in Christ and a mature confidence?

When did you first confess Christ and when did you first grasp what it meant to be committed to Christ?

How does your commitment to Christ relate to the American Dream?

Where does the risk come in, when it comes to discovering the fullness of life in Christ?

DAY 8

Alone, but not Alone

"Do you now believe?" Jesus replied. "A time is coming and in fact has come when you will be scattered, each to your own home. You will leave me all alone. Yet I am not alone, for my Father is with me." John 16:31

Jesus' response has more than a touch of irony. "Oh, right. So now you believe!" Jesus could be reserved about entrusting himself to others, because "he knew all people. He did not need any testimony about mankind, for he knew what was in each person" (John 2:24-25). The disciples believed in him, but did Jesus believe in them? They had faith *in* Jesus but did they have the faith *of* Jesus? Perhaps we all need to hear Jesus say, "Oh, right, So now you believe!" in response to our spiritual mood swings. Mountain-top highs count for little when our daily discipleship is in doubt.

There is more to belief than affirming good ideas. As we have said, to believe is to obey and to obey is to believe. Belief without obedience is cheap grace and obedience without belief is works righteousness. "Costly grace and sacrificial obedience are woven into the tapestry of God's love for us. One cannot be separated from the other without destroying the whole tapestry."[1] Jesus' less than enthusiastic response to the disciples' confession was a reality check. In the upper room Jesus identified his betrayer and warned Peter that he would deny him three times. He informed the disciples that "if the world hates you, keep in mind that it

1. Jim Eschenbrenner, personal correspondence, used with permission.

hated me first" (John 15:18). Jesus gave the disciples a heads-up so they would not be blindsided by persecution. "All this I have told you so that you will not fall away" (John 16:1).

Jesus tried to prevent the disciples from falling away but he predicted that they would be scattered. The distinction between betrayal and denial is important. Treachery and timidity are not the same thing. Frailty is different from faithlessness. In their pre-passion state the disciples were vulnerable; in their post-passion state they would be victorious. Resurrection faith and the power of the Holy Spirit made a profound difference in the boldness of their witness and in the resilience of their faith.

For all their enthusiasm, when the crisis came the disciples scattered. Jesus used the language of the prophet Zechariah to explain their actions, "Strike the shepherd, and the sheep will be scattered . . ." (Zech 13:7; see Mark 14:27). The paradox between falling away and scattering is an important one. When Jesus was arrested in the garden, the disciples panicked and ran, but within hours at least two of them had circled back to get as close as possible to Jesus. John made it as far as the foot of the cross the next day (John 19:26-27).

Under the threat of ISIS many of our brothers and sisters in Christ face the terror of the sword or the shame of denying their Lord. When confronted by a terrorist is it wrong for Christians to pretend to be Muslim by reciting the shahada—Islam's main creed—in Arabic? Some Christians say "yes" because even though they are not denying their devotion to Jesus Christ they are pretending to be something they are not. Others say "no" because Christians are obligated to save their lives. "George Sabra, president of Near East School of Theology in Lebanon, says Christians must rely on the guidance of the Holy Spirit in such situations. Sabra believes that Christians should not say the shahada. But those who do, he says, should be treated with compassion. 'To be a Christian is not about learning tactics for survival,' he said. 'But denying Christ is not an unforgivable sin. We may not despair of

God's love and mercy. Even Peter, the head of the disciples, was a denier of Christ.'"[2]

It is important to note that Jesus is not dependent on his disciples. "You will leave me all alone. Yet I am not alone, for my Father is with me" (John 16:32). This affirms what Jesus said earlier, "The one who sent me is with me; he has not left me alone, for I always do what pleases him" (John 8:29). Jesus has never been the solitary being that we can be, nor has he ever been lonely. The autonomous individual self knows no parallel in his character. The contrast here is between the faithlessness of the disciples and the faithfulness of the Father.[3] The inter-Trinitarian community persists in spite of our faithlessness.

So, there never was a time when Jesus was alone. Never, but one time only, too short to count in the eternity of God, but absolutely essential for our atonement. The poignancy of the truth, "Yet I am not alone, for my Father is with me," only heightens the horror of the abandonment, albeit temporary, that Jesus experienced on the cross when he cried out, "My God, my God, why did you abandon me?!" (Matt 27:46). "But in that Cry should we not balance Jesus' verb 'abandon' which he both meant and felt, with Jesus' *address*, "*My* God, *my* God"?[4]

Reflections on the Way

The disciples didn't fall away, but they did scatter. Have you ever scattered?

How would you pray for Christians who under threat of execution pretend to be a Muslim?

How can we grow in our post-passion resilience?

Can you conceive of any situation that would cause you to abandon your faith in Christ?

2. Casper and Osanjo, "When Christians Say the Shahada," 21.

3. Beasley Murray, *John*, 288.

4. Bruner, *John*, 958.

DAY 9

Take Heart!

"I have told you these things, so that in me you
may have peace. In this world you will have trouble. But take heart! I have overcome the world."
John 16:33

How does the believer take heart? The place to begin is in the
upper room with Jesus. A slow meditative, prayerful reading
of Jesus' discipleship sermon provides the soulful therapy we need
and desire. Jesus told us these things because this knowledge is
essential for living the Christian life. He began with a towel and
basin to illustrate his cleansing atonement and the humble action of discipleship. He brought us into the inner circle to show
us the persistent power of evil. Yet, not even betrayal and denial
can stand in the way of new-commandment love for one another.
Jesus declared, "Do not let your hearts be troubled," and then pro-
ceeded to comfort us with the assurance that he is coming again
and that he is giving us an advocate in the Holy Spirit. He used the
vine and branches to illustrate his abiding presence. In *The God
Who Comforts* we stressed the four-fold nature of Jesus' comfort
in his passion, his Parousia, his Paraclete, and his presence. Jesus
continued the conversation on the streets of Jerusalem as the band
of disciples headed to the Kidron Valley. He reassured them that in
spite of the world's hate "the prince of this world now stands condemned" (John 16:11). "Now is your time of grief," Jesus said, "but
I will see you again and you will rejoice, and no one will take away
your joy" (John 16:22). He warned them that they would scatter,

but that he and the Father remained one. They would desert him for a time but they would not disown him. The Father's devotion would sustain him. The early church confessed:

> If we died with him, we will also live with him;
>
> If we endure we will also reign with him.
>
> If we disown him, he will also disown us;
>
> If we are faithless, he remains faithful, for he cannot disown himself"(2 Tim 2:11-13).

We made the distinction earlier between "falling away" and "scattering," a comparison comparable to the one made in the creed between "disowning" Christ and being "faithless." There is a difference between persistent denial and temporary denial. To deny our Lord and Savior in any way is tragic, but it is not the believer's responsibility to ostracize and shun those Christians who deny their faith in the face of potential martyrdom. My prayer is that I will remain faithful to Christ no matter what the cost, that even if an ISIS terrorist put a knife to my throat I would not deny my Lord. I pray that I'd have the courage of Polycarp, who bravely said, "Eighty and six years I have served him, and he has done me no wrong. How then can I blaspheme my king and Savior?" But with that courage must also come compassion for believers who in their sinful weakness have succumbed to fear and denied Christ. They need not be consigned to a lifelong cause of shame. Jesus made it clear that the unforgivable sin is the persistent, unrepentant rejection of the witness of the Holy Spirit. Jesus said, "Truly I tell you, people can be forgiven all their sins and every slander they utter, but whoever blasphemes against the Holy Spirit will never be forgiven; they are guilty of an eternal sin" (Mark 3:28-29). For a believer to deny the Lord, as Peter did, does not mean that shame must follow him until the end of his life.[1]

We have a responsibility to pray for our brothers and sisters in Christ and to offer to them the grace of Christ. "If you see any brother or sister commit a sin that does not lead to death, you should pray

---

1. Casper and Osanjo, "When Christians Say the Shahada," 21.

and God will give them life" (1 John 5:16). Jesus admonishes us to take heart and that requires some effort on our part. But we are not alone. Spiritual discipline is involved, but our advocate the Holy Spirit will help us stay focused. The author of Hebrews reminds us, "We must pay the most careful attention to what we have heard, so that we do not drift away" (Heb 2:1). The consolation for this effort is the gift of shalom. "Peace I leave with you; my peace I give you" (John 14:27) is the theme that runs through Jesus' upper room discipleship sermon. As we said earlier in our meditation on John 14, we cannot create shalom, any more than we can save ourselves. Jesus makes an important distinction. The true gift of peace is not worldly peace: "My peace I give you. I do not give to you as the world gives." Jesus finishes his discipleship sermon by underscoring in a single word the full measure of his gift to us.

Shalom embraces the fullness of salvation, which means deliverance from "sin and death; guilt and estrangement; ignorance of truth; bondage to habit and vice; fear of demons, of death, of life, of God, of hell; despair of self; alienation from others; pressures of the world; a meaningless life." The meaning of shalom is exceedingly positive, embracing "peace with God, access to God's favor and presence, hope of regaining the glory intended for humankind, endurance in suffering, steadfast character, an optimistic mind, inner motivations of divine love and power of the Spirit, ongoing experience of the risen Christ and sustaining joy in God."[2]

The peace we long for is the peace of God, for only his peace, "which transcends all understanding, will guard [our] hearts and [our] minds in Christ Jesus" (Phil 4:7). This is the lasting peace that survives the pain and suffering of this life and outlasts death itself. "You will keep in perfect peace him whose mind is steadfast, because he trusts in you. Trust in the Lord forever, for the Lord, the Lord himself, is the Rock eternal" (Isa 26:3-4).

The command to courageously take heart is a reminder to daily choose Christ over the world. The world has it own list of peace plans: stoic detachment, consumer distraction, therapeutic

---

2. White, "Salvation," 968.

diversion, pharmaceutical dependence, and hedonistic delight. But none compare to the peace of God.

Reflections on the Way

What stands out to you in Jesus' discipleship sermon?

How should Jesus' patience with the disciples rub off on us?

What worldly peace plan are you most inclined to follow?

How have you taken heart?

Trouble

"In this world you will have trouble. But take
heart! I have overcome the world." John 16:33

We find ourselves living in the midst of two powerful realities:
tribulation and triumph. The word for trouble is the same
word used in John's Revelation for tribulation. The great tribulation
is not only off in the future but here and now. The time of trouble
began at the cross and will end when Christ comes again. In the
mean time the tribulation continues. The Apostle Peter encouraged believers, "Do not be surprised at the painful trial you are
suffering, as though something strange were happening to you"
(1 Pet 4:12). Although the intensity of tribulation may vary, fierce
resistance to the gospel continues and the Christian is called to
remain faithful. Do you believe that living for Christ in this world
inevitably provokes trouble?

The Danish Christian thinker Søren Kierkegaard believed that
there was nothing in the popular Christianity of his day that war-
ranted persecution. Christians were assimilated into the culture so
completely that there was no real difference between a Christian and
a non-Christian. Everyone was a Christian, because no one was a
Christian. The world does not persecute the world when it discovers
itself in Christianity. Christians cannot be at home in the world and
at the same be "a stranger and a pilgrim in the world."[1]

If our lives are basically trouble-free we have either isolated
ourselves from the world or we have conformed to the world. If we

1. Kierkegaard, *Attack Upon 'Christendom,'* 42.

are no longer socially marginalized or ostracized it is because our Christianity is in bland conformity to the world. We no longer need to encourage believers to endure persecution because the world finds nothing in our lives to persecute. We have avoided trouble by conforming a private faith to the indulgences and practices of the world. Our ethics are shaped by the spirit of the times and our lifestyle reflects the values and priorities of our non-Christian neighbors. We go to church a couple of times a month and may even tithe our income, but we spend much more on ourselves than on the mission of the church. The only time we open our Bible is in church and we don't pray very much because we just don't and we are inclined to blame God when things don't go our way.

Jesus said, "In this world you will have trouble." The trouble he had in mind was not simply an illness or an accident or a difficult family situation. It was not the hectic pace one may be expected to keep at work or a frustration of personal ambition. It is not increased mortgage rates. Nor is the trouble some inward psychological feeling or depression. We trivialize the tribulation if we define it according to an array of everyday calamities that come upon us, irrespective of our commitment to Christ and his kingdom. The troubles Jesus referred to have a more definite, specifically Christian meaning. His prediction of trouble rules out any superficial equating of negative circumstances with the practical reality of taking up our cross and following Jesus.

If what Jesus said on the eve of his crucifixion is true, we should not be surprised to experience trouble in the world. We know our hope is not in America or in any kind of political policy or economic system. Yet some Christians talk as if they had no other identity or loyalty other than to America. Their vitriolic rhetoric and slander is an indication not of strength and boldness, but of fear and hate. Frustrated Christians feel that their culture is slipping away from them in spite of their best efforts to "bring back America" and "change the world for Christ." We need to hear what Jesus said to Pilate over and over again to stay on mission: "My kingdom is not of this world. If it were, my servants would fight to prevent my arrest by the Jewish leaders. But now my kingdom is from another place" (John 18:36). The gospel is a unique countercultural movement, a voice crying in the wilderness of an evil and broken culture. The people of God should never expect to be the controlling voice of culture, but they should aim to impress the world with Christ's love and goodness.

The apostles took Jesus at his word: "I have overcome the world." They had not been given "a spirit of timidity, but a spirit of power, of love and of self discipline" (2 Tim 1:7). God is in control. The victory of Christ is assured. We entrust ourselves to the providence of God. Patient endurance and faithfulness rule out revenge and retaliation. The world should never have to fear a Christian. Those who persecute, insult, threaten, slander, swindle, and murder Christians are never in danger of receiving the same treatment they perpetrate and perpetuate. Christians defend others and themselves from violence, slander, deception, and terrorism, but the disciple of the Lord Jesus Christ does not fight the way the world does. "For though we live in the world, we do not wage war as the world does. The weapons we fight with are not the weapons of the world" (2 Cor 10:4). We don't fight fire with fire and render evil for evil because of the victory of the cross and the power of the resurrection.

"At the end," writes missionary statesman Lesslie Newbigin, "the triumph song of the Church will not be 'We have overcome' but 'Worthy is the Lamb that was slain' (Rev 5:12). The life of the Church will thus be a strange paradox—the peace which is the mark of God's victorious reign enjoyed here and now in the midst of the battle with the powers of this world. Precisely these tribulations, the mark of the final conflict between the kingdom of God and the powers of the world, will be the mark of those who already enjoy in foretaste the peace of God's victory."[2]

2. Newbigin, *The Light Has Come*, 222.

Reflections on the Way

What kind of trouble should Christians expect?

Why is our song not "We Shall Overcome"?

How do you know that you are dependent on the peace of Christ?

Why should the world never have to fear a Christian?

DAY 11

Raised Eyes

"After Jesus said this, he looked toward heaven
and prayed. . ." John 17:1

We made so much of Jesus getting down on his knees to wash
the disciples' feet that we cannot ignore Jesus looking up
to pray. Humility and adoration provide the right posture for
true spirituality and frame this pre-crucifixion prayer. In a parable, Jesus contrasted the proud Pharisee with the repentant tax
collector who "would not even look up to heaven" (Luke 18:13).
Unlike the prayer of the tax collector, Jesus' prayer is not a prayer
of repentance. Even so, Jesus has humbled himself on his knees
and is about to humble himself on the cross. His previous actions
give this exalted prayer its true reference: "For all those who exalt
themselves will be humbled, and those who humble themselves
will be exalted" (Luke 18:14).

Jesus looked up to pray, not within to reflect. His prayer was
not an inner dialogue, the kind we have with ourselves, between
me, myself, and I, but a real conversation with the Father. Jesus
prayed because he was one with the Father in his deity and because he was one with us in our humanity. Precisely because Jesus
is God, communion between the Father and the Son during Jesus'
earthly ministry makes perfect sense. His prayer life reflects his
eternal oneness with the Father before the worlds were formed.
Jesus' praying does not make him less than God or any less worthy
of our prayers today. Recognized as one of the most influential
theologians of the early Greek church, Origen advised believers,

> Now if we are to take prayer in its most exact sense, perhaps we should not pray to anyone begotten, not even to Christ Himself, but only the God and Father of all, to whom even our Savior himself prayed. For when he heard, 'teach us to pray,' he did not teach us to pray to himself, but to the Father by saying, "Our Father in heaven. . . ."

Origen concluded that we should not "pray to someone else who prays, but rather to the Father whom our Lord Jesus taught us to address in prayers. . . .For you must not pray to the High Priest appointed on your behalf by the Father (Heb 8:3) or to the Advocate who is charged by the Father with praying to you (1 John 2:1). Rather you must pray through the Holy Spirit and Advocate."[1] Origen created an artificial distinction between Jesus' human experience of God and the eternal Son's communion with the Father. Because Jesus prayed to the Father and counseled others to pray to the Father, Origen drew the unwarranted conclusion that Jesus' prayer life was indicative of his eternal subordination. He argued that prayer should be addressed to the Father alone through the Son. Origen's outlook is contradicted by the fact that Jesus is one with the Father. His prayer life was "not merely a necessity of communication occasioned by the flesh" but a demonstration of the "intimacy of communion brought into the flesh."[2] In this first sense Jesus' prayer life demonstrated the eternal interdependence between God the Father and God the Son. A second way to understand Jesus' prayer life complements the first and takes seriously the incarnation. Jesus prays out of human necessity. The prayer life of Jesus shows us his full dependence upon the Father as a human being and his interdependence with the Father as God the Son.

For Jesus the line between communion with his Father and conversation with his disciples was very thin. Dialogue and devotion went hand in hand. This was especially evident following Jesus' entry into Jerusalem. We see a close affinity between what

1. Origen, *An Exhortation to Martyrdom, Prayer and Selected Works*, 112-13.

2. Anderson, *Historical Transcendence and the Reality of God*, 178.

Jesus said to his disciples and what he prayed to his Father: "The hour has come for the Son of Man to be glorified . . . Now my soul is troubled, and what shall I say? 'Father, save me from this hour'? No, it was for this very reason I came to this hour. 'Father, glorify your name!'" (John 12:23, 27-28). John frames Jesus' entire discipleship sermon with prayers that point forward to Jesus' Glory prayer and his Gethsemane prayer. If Cotton Mather could say, "My life is almost a continual conversation with Heaven," how much more could the Son.[3] His example inspires us to ask how thin the line is between our praying and our living. To pray is to live and to live is to pray.

The reason we have this prayer is because Jesus prayed *with* and *for* the disciples. He might have prayed in silence, but he chose to include his disciples and us in his prayer. Augustine observed that Jesus, "the Lord, the Only-begotten and co-eternal with the Father," wanted to show his disciples that he prayed to the Father, "that He might remember that he was still our Teacher."[4] The discourse ended but the means of edification continued.

It is reasonable to conclude that we have Jesus' prayer verbatim for several reasons. First, the disciples listened to Jesus carefully. They would have followed the prayer's three main sections easily. Jesus prayed for himself (1-5), for his disciples (6-19), and for the church (20-26).[5] Second, the similarity between this prayer and the Lord's Prayer may have also made it easier to remember. Dale Bruner calls it, "The Lord's 'Lord's Prayer.'"[6] He identifies six parallel petitions:

The Lord's Prayer // The Lord's 'Lord's Prayer'

Our Father, in heaven // Jesus lifted his eyes to heaven and said, Father (17:1a)

3. Kennedy, *The First American Evangelical*, 129.
4. Augustine, *Homilies on the Gospel of John*, 394.
5. Beasley-Murray, *John*, 295.
6. Bruner, *John*, 960.

Hallowed be your name // Glorify your Son so that the Son may glorify you (17:1b, 4-5)

Your kingdom come // Holy Father, keep them in your name that you gave to me, so that they may be one as we are one (17:11

Your will be done // Keep them from the Evil One (17:15b)

On earth as it is in heaven // I am not asking you to take them out of the world (17:15a)

Give us today our daily bread // Sanctify them in the truth; your Word is truth (17:17)

And forgive our debts as we have forgiven our debtors // May they all be one [as we are one],so that the world may believe (17:21)

Lead us not into temptation but deliver us from the Evil One // Father, I want the community you gave me to be with me where I am (17:24).

Third, the simplicity of the vocabulary and Jesus' conversational style make it easy to remember. "This chapter is the easiest in the whole Scripture as regards the words, the deepest in meaning."[7] It is an easy prayer to take down, but its meaning is impossible to exhaust. Lesslie Newbigin writes, "The prayer leads us into the very heart of the ministry and message of Jesus, and no exposition can hope to do more than suggest some aspects of its meaning."[8] Fourth, the disciples' conversation among themselves and with Jesus after the resurrection provided ample opportunity to get it right. Finally, and maybe the most important reason, the gift of the Holy Spirit was given to help the disciples recall the words of Jesus (John 16:13).[9]

Although Jesus diverted his eyes from the disciples and focused his attention on the Father, all of his disciples past and

---

7. Ibid., 964. Quoting Johannes Albrecht Bengel.

8. Newbigin, *The Light Has Come*, 223.

9. Bruner, *John*, 966.

present are meant to enter into this prayer. The thin line between communion with the Father and community with his disciples makes us part of this prayer. We long to grasp the meaning of Jesus' longest prayer, to linger on the simple words, to meditate on their profound meaning, and to pray *with* Jesus, even as he prays *for* us.

Reflections on the Way

Why did Jesus pray and why do we pray?

How is prayer different from getting in touch with our feelings?

What do you think of the comparison between the Lord's Prayer and the Gethsemane prayer?

How can you enter into Jesus' prayer?

DAY 12

The Hour

"Father, the hour has come." John 17:1

We know the difference between an hour-long business meeting and a metaphor that stands for one of life's defining moments. The ticking down of sixty minutes holds no comparison to the critical hour when the meaning of life is on the line. On June 18, 1940, British Prime Minister Winston Churchill announced the Battle of Britain. After assessing the strength of the army, navy, and air force, Churchill affirmed "the resolve of Britain and the British Empire to fight on." He concluded his thirty-minute speech with these words, "Let us therefore brace ourselves to our duty, and so bear ourselves that if the British Empire and Commonwealth lasts for a thousand years, men will still say, 'This was their finest hour.'"[1]

Throughout his earthly ministry Jesus was conscious that salvation history was about to climax in this hour. John's reference to the *hour* is one of seven deep meaning indicators given in the introduction to the upper room.[2] The upper room experience from beginning to end is framed by God's special grace-filled *kairos* timing. "Jesus knew that the hour had come for him to leave this world and go to the Father" (John 13:1). At the outset of his public ministry, at the wedding feast of Cana, Jesus revealed his consciousness of God's special timing when he said to his mother, "My hour has

1. http://www.winstonchurchill.org/resources/speeches/1940-the-finest-hour/122-the-finest-hour.

2. Webster, *The God Who Kneels*, 23.

45

not come" (John 2:4). At Jacob's well, Jesus said to the Samaritan, "Woman, believe me, an hour is coming when you will worship the Father neither on this mountain nor in Jerusalem. . . .Yet an hour is coming and has now come when the true worshipers will worship the Father in the Spirit and the truth . . ." (John 4:21, 23). In defending his authority and power, Jesus said to the religious leaders, "Very truly I tell you, an hour is coming and has now come when the dead will hear the voice of the Son of God and those who hear will live" (John 5:25). The "already but not yet" nature of this pending *hour* affirms the meaning of Jesus' ministry in the light of the cross and the resurrection. The impact of the hour was already being felt but the significance of the hour would not be fully accomplished until after Christ's passion. When his brothers badgered him about going up to Jerusalem for the festival, Jesus told them, "My time is not yet here; for you any time will do" (John 7:6). But Jesus ended up going to the festival and teaching in the temple, and causing such a stir that the religious leaders tried to seize him. John writes, "no one laid a hand on him, because his hour had not yet come" (John 7:30; see 8:20).

Then, shortly before Thursday night, Jesus declared publicly, "The hour has come for the Son of Man to be glorified" (John 12:23). He shared personally how the impact of this announcement made him feel, "Now my soul is troubled, and what shall I say? 'Father, save me from this hour'? No, it was for this very reason I came to this hour. 'Father, glorify your name!'" (John 12:27). He was keenly aware of the pending passion and the sacrifice he was about to make. Now, with his discipleship sermon complete, Jesus raises his eyes to heaven and prays, "Father, it's time."

Jesus prayed to the "Father" at the beginning and then to the "Righteous Father" at the end (John 17:25). In so doing he signified the intimate and trusting nature of his conversation with the Father throughout. Jesus is not only in sync with the Father's will, he is one with the Father in his very being. We read in Hebrews that, "The Son is the radiance of God's glory and the exact representation of his being, sustaining all things by his powerful word" (Heb 1:3). Jesus uses the simple address, "Father," and encourages us to do the same (Luke 11:2; Matt 6:9). The next line in Hebrews reads, "After he had provided purification for sins, he sat down at the right hand of the Majesty in heaven" (Heb 1:3). So between these two lines, "The Son is the radiance of God's glory . . ." and "After he had provided purification for sins . . ." we have Jesus' Prayer of Consecration and the entire passion unfolds. The finished work of Christ is all but done; the only thing left was to actually do it. But as far as Jesus is concerned he has reached the finish line. His simple statement suggests calm resolve rather than resignation. The hour and all that it involved and all that it accomplished is an objective matter of fact. Judging from his focus on glory, authority, eternal life, and his finished work, faithfulness, not fate, propels him forward. This hour has been a long time coming, but now thank God it has arrived. Gratitude is the subtext of Jesus' prayer. He is conscious of Father's approval and commitment (John 12:28). He has the Father's backing. He is in the center of the Father's will.

We mark the passing of time with birthdays, graduations, anniversaries, and memorial services. We celebrate notable achievements. We honor those who retire after a long career. Every spring a pastor friend of mine in Nebraska is invited to a score of high school graduation parties to honor the seniors who have reached a milestone. All of these special days are an occasion to gather family and friends together and celebrate the people we love. In addition, we mark our calendars with the start of school in late August, followed by Thanksgiving, Christmas, New Year's Day, Easter, and summer vacation. The older we get the faster we seem to cycle through these *chronos* seasons. My wife's eighty-year-old uncle, a physician with a busy practice, commented this past year, "The days are long and the years are short."

Our special days are important, but they hardly compare to Jesus' hour. Surely nothing we do compares to his *hour* and what he accomplished for us. His once for all atoning sacrifice for our sins stands alone in significance and timing. Nevertheless he invites us to take up our cross *daily* and follow him. He penetrates the linear stream of *chronos* time with grace-filled *kairos* significance. In Christ, we acquire a sense of timing that corresponds to God's timing: special moments uniquely marked by the expectation and fulfillment of God's will and purpose for our lives. Jesus calls each one of us to take up our cross and follow him. For the sake of Christ and his kingdom we experience our own passion narrative. The repetitive cycle of time gives way to those *kairos* moments when it seems that time itself stands still. The linear line of *chronos* time is punctuated by the pulsing heartbeat of meaning. We are truly alive and engaged with the mission of God. Jesus never said the *hour* would be easy. It will look and feel much more like a crucifixion than an awards ceremony. But instead of putting in time we will be filling up in real time "what is still lacking in regard to Christ's afflictions, for the sake of his body, which is the church" (Col 1:24). For the followers of Jesus Christ this is their finest hour.

Reflections on the Way

Describe a *kairos* moment in your life?

In what sense was Jesus' hour absolutely unique to him?

How does the command to take up our cross daily and follow Jesus identify with his hour?

What does it mean for believers to have a passion narrative?

Jesus' Glory Prayer

"Glorify your Son, that your Son may glorify you." John 17:1

Jesus' glory prayer begins with a prayer of personal consecration. He is about to pray for his present and future disciples, but before he prays for us, he prays for himself. He models in his own prayer the complete dependence on the will of the Father that he expects of all of his disciples. His first petition echoes his earlier confession: "Very truly I tell you, the Son can do nothing by himself; he can do only what he sees the Father doing . . ." (John 5:19). First his request, "Glorify your Son," and then his antiphonal response, "that your Son may glorify you," reiterate the reciprocal concert between Father and Son that has been playing out in the Gospels. Jesus has been showing us how to pray, "Hallowed be Your Name," and mean it.

His prayer request is simple, "Father, glorify your name!" and "a voice from heaven" declares, "I have glorified it, and will glorify it again" (John 5:28). We are not used to so much pre-passion, earthly "glory" but the glory is there and has been there from the beginning. We don't have to wait until Easter morning to behold the glory. John has been showing us God's glory and honor right along in the grace and truth of Jesus. "The Word was made flesh and dwelt among us and we beheld his glory, the glory of the only begotten of the Father, full of grace and truth" (John 1:14). "The single major way that the Father's name is glorified on earth" is by "the honoring of his Son, who is the Father's authorized

Self-Representation."[1] Dale Bruner reflects in practical terms what lies behind Jesus' glory prayer.

> *"Father, please help me to say and to do the right things this decisive Weekend; give me the strength and wisdom to go through the trials and the Cross just ahead so that I can make a full and clean atonement for the whole world's sins, as you and I so deeply want. And then especially, Father, please raise me up again after I am put to death in order definitely to conquer death and to show the world, decisively and comfortingly, that death has, in fact and not just in myth, been conquered in history. I want this Weekend to be everything you and I hoped it would be for the world and for the Church, the bearer of our message to the world. Please help me and them."[2]*

Have you ever wanted a weekend to go just right? It may be a wedding or a family reunion or a big game, but you did everything in your power to prepare for a good outcome. You wanted everything just perfect. These special occasions rarely come together like we hoped they would, but when they do they are fixed in our memory as very special. I don't think our two married sons will mind if I bask a little in the glory of their sister's wedding. Our daughter's wedding seemed to sum up all the goodness and joy of our church experience in San Diego. The whole church was invited and so many pitched it to make the worship and the reception truly special that it stands out as the summa cum laude experience of our fourteen years of pastoral ministry in the city. Family and friends came in from around the country, and people opened their homes in hospitality. The weather was perfect. The informal rehearsal dinner was a whole lot of fun with laughter, music and Phil's Barbecue. Our church family showed their love for us in the way they entered into that special day. Everything about the marriage ceremony, the radiant bride, the joy of the wedding party, the music, the prayers, the Scripture meditation, and the exchange of vows flowed together as if it were a single worship-filled moment.

1. Bruner, *John*, 967.
2. Bruner, *John*, 967

I have a beautiful picture of a happy congregation surrounding a joyful bride and groom in the church courtyard that was taken during the reception. For me the joy of that perfect day is a faint foretaste of the marriage supper of the Lamb.

Jesus wanted the weekend to go just right, but for him perfection meant giving his life as an atoning sacrifice for our sins. To pray the way he prayed meant that he embraced the will of the Father *passionately*. Like a bride eager to experience everything about her wedding day, Jesus was all in and he proved it by praying his glory prayer. Jesus showed he was the Son "who is the radiance of God's glory" by how he prayed (Heb 1:3). He gave us a model for our own consecration. We enter into God's will by praying the way Jesus prayed, "Glorify me that I might glorify You." This is the glory-prayer that captures the passion of Abraham, knife in hand standing over Isaac. This is the prayer that Job prayed on the ash heap and the prayer that Isaiah prayed, when he said, "Here I am, send me." The prayer of consecration is a prayer that acknowledges our utter dependence upon our heavenly Father to accomplish his will through us.

Until Jesus proved otherwise we would never have associated glorification with crucifixion but that is precisely what happened in Christ's life and what happens figuratively in our lives. When Judas left the upper room, Jesus spoke of the true meaning of glory: "Now the Son of Man is glorified and God is glorified in him. If God is glorified in him, God will glorify the Son in himself, and will glorify him at once" (John 13:31-32). Paradoxically, the cross stands as a blatant symbol of evil and wretchedness, but the cross also stands as a powerful symbol of God's glory. The cross of Jesus represents unspeakable cruelty, but it is also incredibly glorious, because it is the ultimate demonstration of God's love. We see Jesus, "now crowned with glory and honor because he suffered death, so that by the grace of God he might taste death for everyone" (Heb 2:9).

We are in the habit of associating glory with an overwhelming aesthetic experience in nature. At the base of Mount Rainer on a beautiful day we are compelled to exclaim, "The whole earth is full of his glory" (Isa 6:3). When we hold a newborn baby, we feel like angels are watching and we pray the psalms, "You have made her a little lower than the angels and crowned her with glory and honor" (Ps 8:5).

We also associate glory with brightness, splendor, and luminosity.[3] Glory is something to be seen. The psalmist declares, "The Lord reigns. . . . and all peoples see his glory" (Ps 97:1, 6). Isaiah writes, "They will see the glory of the Lord, the splendor of our God" (Isa 35:2). In Ezekiel's vision the temple court is "full of the radiance of the glory of the Lord" (Ezek 10:4). When the angel of the Lord appeared to the shepherds "the glory of the Lord shone around them, and they were terrified" (Luke 2:9). Moments before Stephen was martyred he looked up to heaven and saw "the glory of God, and Jesus standing at the right hand of God" (Acts 7:55). The Apostle John describes the Holy City "coming down out of heaven from God. It shone with the glory of God, and its brilliance was like that of a very precious jewel, like a jasper, clear as crystal. . . . The city does not need the sun or the moon to shine on it, for the glory of God gives it light, and the Lamb is its lamp" (Rev 21:10-11, 23).

The Old Testament meaning of glory (kāvôd) is related to a verb meaning "to be heavy" (kāvēd).[4] Glory belongs to that which is *weighty*, conveying the idea of *importance, significance, and preeminence*. The psalms emphasize this aspect of God's glory: "Lift up your heads, you gates; be lifted up, you ancient doors, that the King of glory may come in. Who is this King of glory? The Lord strong and mighty . . ." (Ps 24:7-8). True worshipers "declare his glory among the nations and his marvelous deeds among all peoples" (Ps 96:3). Influential people have a certain gravitas, pulling people into their orbit like the earth in orbit around the sun. But there is no one with greater gravitas and greater glory than the Son who is the radiance of God's glory (Heb 1:3). We never would have imagined that the weightiness of God's glory would be revealed at the cross. But God's love dictates that crucifixion

3. Lewis, *The Weight of Glory*, 16.
4. Ross, *Recalling the Hope of Glory*, 46.

and glorification meet here for our salvation. "In bringing many sons and daughters to glory, it was fitting that God, for whom and through whom everything exists, should make the pioneer of their salvation perfect through what he suffered" (Heb 2:10). This is why the apostle said, "May I never boast except in the cross of our Lord Jesus Christ, through which the world has been crucified to me, and I to the world" (Gal 6:14).

Reflections on the Way

Why should we expect to see the glory of God on this side of heaven?

How did the Father glorify the Son?

Reflect on ways that you have experienced the glory of God.

How does an understanding of God's glory impact daily discipleship?

All

"For you granted him authority over all people
that he might give eternal life to all those you
have given him." John 17:2

Jesus' prayer of self-consecration rests on the gospel. The first petition, "Glorify your Son, that your Son may glorify you," is locked in to the second petition. "Hallowed by your name" cannot be separated from "Your Kingdom come, your will be done." The glory of God is reflected in the gospel and the gospel is the result of the glory of God. Jesus is praying "that the Father's will may be done in him."[1] Earlier we referred to the thin line between Jesus' conversation with the disciples and his communion with the Father. Just moments ago, Jesus affirmed in creedal form the pivotal events of the Gospel: "I came from the Father" (mission); "I entered the world" (nativity/incarnation); "I am leaving the world" (the passion); "I am going back to the Father" (ascension). Now Jesus affirms in confessional form the substance of the gospel: The Father has given the Son all authority over all people in order to give eternal life to all those the Father has given him. Jesus' farewell prayer defines in gospel terms the second and third petition of the Lord's Prayer, "Your kingdom come, your will be done." The kingdom of God is the rule and reign of Christ and the will of God is for all people to know the only true God through Jesus Christ.

Jesus' prayer of consecration makes no claim of self-importance or solo action. The Son can do nothing apart from the

1. Morris, *John*, 717.

Father and everything he does is in the Father's will. The Father has granted him all authority over all people that he might give eternal life to all those you have given him. There is synergy between the Father's giving and the Son's giving, between the Father's authority and the Son's authority. They act in tandem—they act as one—and we are the beneficiaries of their deep communion.

All Authority, All People, All Saints—There is a striking affinity between Jesus' prayer of consecration and his great commission to the disciples. The first of three *alls* is implied in his prayer but stated explicitly at his ascension. Jesus said, "*All* authority in heaven and on earth has been given to me. Therefore go and make disciples of *all* nations, baptizing them in the name of the Father and of the Son and of the Holy Spirit, and teaching them to obey everything I have commanded you. And surely I am with you *always*, to the very end of the age" (Matt 28:18-20).

The scope and meaning of Jesus' authority is celebrated by the Apostle Paul on the grandest scale with a noticeable emphasis on this little word *all*.

> The Son is the image of the invisible God, the firstborn over *all* creation. For in him *all* things were created: things in heaven and on earth, visible and invisible, whether thrones or powers or rulers or authorities; *all* things have been created through and for him. He is before *all* things, and in him *all* things hold together. And he is the head of the body, the church; he is the beginning and the firstborn from among the dead, so that in *everything* he might have the supremacy. For God was pleased to have *all* his fullness dwell in him, and through him to reconcile to himself *all* things, whether things on earth or things in heaven, by making peace through his blood, shed on the cross (Col 1:15-20).

The apostle challenges us to embrace the invisible reality of God in Christ reconciling the world to himself. We are so easily tempted to reduce everything down to the small world of self-realization and self-discovery. Give us comfort, convenience, and entertainment and we are happy campers. May it not be so! There is nothing small or individualistic about the authority of Jesus. The Author/ Artist/Composer of all creation and the Savior/Redeemer/Lord of all salvation are one and the same. The history of nature and the history of redemption are revelations of the same God. Each reinforces the wonder, awe, beauty, and truth of the other. The God and Father of our Lord Jesus Christ, who authored DNA and ordained redemption, has purposed "to bring unity to all things in heaven and on earth under Christ" (Eph 1:10).

The gospel of Christ supports this inclusive, all-encompassing understanding of truth as well. Jesus affirmed the reality of total truth when he said, "I am the way and the truth and the life. No one comes to the Father except through me" (John 14:6). All of life is of God and belongs to God. Creation and redemption converge to infuse life with sacred significance. "He is before all things, and in him all things hold together" and all things are reconciled through him, "by making peace through his blood shed on the cross." The Divine purpose—bringing unity to all things in heaven and on earth in Christ, overcomes the great divorce between our fallenness and our fulfillment. In Christ the physical and the spiritual, the temporal and the eternal, the mundane and the devotional are united. Redemptive love rescues romantic love, integrates truth and beauty, unifies families and races, and infuses meaning in ordinary daily life. This unity depends on the absolute singularity of Christ.

The simple word *all* with its all-encompassing reality is the key. Unless we embrace the truth of this tiny word, we will never know the health and wholeness of an undivided heart and mind. Jesus is Lord of *all*; all creation is his by right of inheritance, design, creation and redemption. The tremendous truth of this confession is that in Christ we participate in this *all*. This is the *all* that must not be evaded but embraced by all who desire to please God, because God's holy claim rests equally on all. So that "whatever we do, whether in word or deed, we do it all in the name of the Lord Jesus, giving thanks to God the Father through him" (Col 3:17). This is the *all* that believes that Jesus accomplished *all* on the Cross. Judging from a worldly perspective, Jesus' life ended in tragic failure on the cross. In that moment, all was lost, hopelessly lost. Yet from an eternal perspective, Jesus "had in the same moment accomplished all, and on that account said, with eternity's wisdom, 'It is finished.'"[2]

This is the *all* that is willing to *suffer all* for God. This is the *all* of a covenant love that is grandly inclusive of all we are and will be. This is the all-encompassing commitment to love and serve Christ, worship and cherish him in prosperity and in adversity; in sorrow and in happiness; in sickness and in health; and forsaking all others, be united to him for all eternity. This is the *all* that knows no limits.

> He who did not spare his own Son,
> but gave him up for us all —
> how will he not also, along with him,
> graciously give us all things? (Rom 8:32).

Reflections on the Way

What is the relationship between authority and love in Jesus?

Why are we so tempted to be our own authority?

What is the downside to overlooking this little word "all"?

What does it mean for our commitment to Christ to be all encompassing?

2. Kierkegaard, *Purity of Heart*, 138.

The Gospel

"Now this is eternal life: that they know you, the
only true God, and Jesus Christ, whom you have
sent." John 17:3

Simply stated the gospel is the assurance of eternal life, that is
"deep, lasting life," through knowing "the only true God, and
Jesus Christ, his Self-Representative."[1] The greatest offense of the
gospel is its exclusive truth claim. It may be the single most difficult issue confronting both believer and unbeliever. Even modern
objections against the miraculous and soul-searching questions
about pain and suffering seem to pale in significance, when compared to the claim made by Jesus, "I am the way, the truth, and the
life, no one comes to the Father except through me."

Living as we do in the "global village," Christians are reminded daily that there are many alternatives to Jesus. In an age
of choice it is popular to believe that there are many ways to God.
Many claim that truth is no longer fixed but fluid; it is whatever
you say it is. What matters most is how the truth feels—what is
true for you may not be true for me. Jesus is just one of many ways
to be spiritual, to acknowledge the transcendent one. Though
other religions may claim to be the only way, most do not, creating
the impression that evangelical Christians are more like militant
Muslims than reasonable, sensible people.

One of the heroes of the twentieth century, Mahatma Gan-
dhi, offered his conclusion to the matter in an essay entitled *All*

1. Bruner, *John*, 971.

Religions Are True. That idea appears to be growing in acceptance. For many it seems only reasonable to conclude that the eternal one is perceived differently in different cultures, because whatever we mean by "God" exceeds the scope of human thought, language, and experience. The global village shares different and distinctive religious perceptions of the one transcendent reality.

The apostles clearly understood the absolute claim of Jesus and declared, "Salvation is found in no one else, for there is no other name under heaven given to people by which we must be saved" (Acts 4:12). The early church was convinced that Jesus was the revelation of God, the culmination of a long history of revelation, the very self-disclosure of God. The exclusive truth claim of the gospel fits with the purpose of God's promise from the beginning. God chose one, small, weak, insignificant nation through which to make himself known and bless the world. The exclusiveness of the gospel is consistent with the character of revelation and the nature of God's own self-disclosure.

There are not many gods to know, as the Canaanites or the Greeks or Hindus believed, but only one God. All the rest are idols. Neither is God a vague abstraction; a nameless, undefined, indistinguishable being or force or feeling or projection. God's self-disclosure is more definite, definable, specific and singular than we can fully grasp—more than we can completely comprehend, not less! If we consider our own personhood distinctive and unique, how could God, the very author of life, and the maker of the universe, be any less? If our sense of self recoils at the notion of being just one of the masses, we can be assured that the Lord God is no less the person that we are. There is in fact only one you! And there is in truth only one God! The Word of God declares, "I am the Lord your God . . . You shall have no other gods before me . . . You shall not make for yourself an idol" (Exod 20:3-4). "Hear, O Israel: The Lord our God, the Lord is one. Love the Lord your God with all your heart and with all your soul and with all your strength" (Deut 6:4-5).

The apostles believed that the promise of God given to Abraham, that "all the peoples on earth will be blessed through you," is fulfilled in Jesus. And each subsequent stage of salvation history, from Moses to the Prophets, from David to Jeremiah, anticipated the Savior; not an ethnic Savior, not a cultural religion, not a tribal deity, but the Savior of the world. "For God so loved the world that he gave his one and only Son . . ." (John 3:16). The one and only way makes sense because of the one and only Son!

Since this little creed is in the third person some scholars suggest it might have been an editor's footnote or a bracketed statement if such literary options had been available to John. Others attribute the confession directly to Jesus himself. Even though it is the Lord's Lord's Prayer it is still a model for all disciples to pray. Our self-consecration, like our Lord's, is based exclusively on the gospel. Jesus was intensely personal with the Father but also wholly intentional about praying with and for the disciples. Verse one can easily become our prayer of consecration by changing only one word: "Father, the hour has come. Glorify your *servant*, that your *servant* may glorify you." Previous generations tended to pray in the third person as a sign of humility. They echoed the Psalms by referring to themselves as "your servant." The use the third person reflects the humility of the incarnation and the truth of the exaltation.

Although Jesus used the first person with the disciples ("I entered the world . . .") and the third person with the Father ("For you granted him. . .) we need not conclude that this was an insertion added by John. Jesus referred to himself in the third person as the Son of Man often in his teaching (John 12:23) and he does so here in his prayer to emphasize the authority of the Father and the meaning of the gospel. Jesus' prayer reflects the deeply felt intimacy and humility that has characterized the Son in relationship with the Father from the beginning.

In some cultures addressing one's master in the third person is a sign of humility. We see instances of this in the Psalms. David switches from the first person, "To you, Lord, I call; you are my Rock," to the third person, "The Lord is the strength of his people, a fortress of salvation for his *anointed one*" (Ps 28:1, 8). In Psalm 68, David begins, "You, God, are my God, earnestly I seek you," and concludes in the third person, "But the *king* will rejoice in God . . ." (Ps 68:1, 11). More importantly we have instances in the Old Testament of Yahweh referring to himself as Yahweh, as when Yahweh stood with Moses and proclaimed his name, "the name Yahweh" (Exod 34:5). Psalm 110 is an important example, "The Lord says to my Lord: 'Sit at my right hand until I make your enemies a footstool for your feet'" (Ps 110:1).

Biblical scholar Andrew Malone cites a revealing list of "third-person self-references and Trinitarian hints in the Old Testament."[2] The way Yahweh spoke of himself is not unlike Jesus' referring to himself as "Jesus Christ." For example, Yahweh said to Moses, "I will cause all my goodness to pass in front of you, and I will proclaim my name, the Lord, in your presence" (Exod 33:19). Or when Yahweh said to David, "The Lord declares to you that the Lord himself will establish a house for you . . ." (2 Sam 7:11). These divine self-references help to establish a precedent for Jesus' third-person self-reference. When he refers to himself in the third person he is not distancing himself from his identity, but humbly confessing the true meaning of the gospel.

Reflections on the Way

Although it may be difficult to accept, why does the exclusive truth-claim of the gospel make sense?

How can Christians commend the truth of the gospel to a skeptical world?

What part does prayer play in seeking and saving the lost?

What does it mean for Jesus to speak of himself in the third person?

2. Malone, "God The Illeist," 501.

True Glory

"I have brought you glory on earth by finishing
the work you gave me to do. And now, Father, glorify me in your presence with the glory I had with
you before the world began." John 17:4-5

Jesus gives a new and distinctive meaning to glory. The original
Greek word *doxa* or *doxazō* meant opinion, conjecture, or repu-
tation. It had a broad meaning ranging from what people thought
of someone to one's own sense of self-esteem. In the Greek version of the Old Testament, the Septuagint, the word doxa became
associated with the Hebrew concept of *kābôd* and referred specifically to the weighty or luminous revelation (influence) of God.
What is important to see is that the popular and broadly based
understanding of glory took on a specific and transcendent meaning in reference to God.[1] Bruce Springsteen's ode to high school
"Glory Days" captures the ancient Greek sentiment. John Legend's
anthem "Glory," sung in the movie *Selma*, deepens the meaning to
include the victory of social justice achieved through self-sacrifice.
But the song's reference to the "coming of the Lord" is best defined
not as our humanitarian effort, but as the finished work of Christ
on the cross.

The consummation of the Father's will is so certain that Jesus
prays as if the passion had already happened. And in one sense
it already had, since every ounce of energy, every fiber of his being, was committed to the cross. As Augustine says, "he knew with

1. Aalen, "Glory," 44-45.

perfect certainty that he would finish" the work committed unto him to do.[2] Since Jesus brought the Father "glory on earth," he now prays for the glory that he had with the Father "before the world began." Jesus links the glory of the cross and the glory of the pre-existent Son of God. Only in the mind of God could these two glories be linked. The glory of the God who so loved the world that he gave his one and only Son and the glory of the Son who made himself nothing . . . being made in human likeness (Phil 2:7) unite at the cross. The author of Hebrews also links these two glories: "The Son is the radiance of God's glory. . . . After he had provided purification for sins, he sat down at the right hand of the Majesty in heaven" (Heb 1:3).

When Harvard was founded in 1636, it was dedicated, "*In Christi Gloriam*" ("To the Glory of Christ"). The Harvard coat of arms depicted three open books representing the Trinity, God the Father, Son, and Holy Spirit. The image of the book represented the Bible. Seven years later the inscription was changed from "To the glory of Christ," to simply "*Veritas*" (Truth) as a shorthand way of recognizing Jesus Christ as the ultimate truth. However, the meaning of the coat of arms kept changing over time. The three books no longer represented the triune God, but the university's task of training ministers, magistrates, and merchants in the three languages of antiquity: Hebrew, Greek, and Latin. The meaning of "*Veritas*" changed as well, from the truth in Christ to a broader concept of generic truth.

The words of Jesus are carved in stone at the University of Chicago, "You shall know the truth and the truth shall set you free," but today it is not the truth of Jesus that is being honored in the motto. It is rather, the modern notion of "truth" as an elusive goal, the endless search without a final destination. Pilate's "What is truth?" would be a more timely and honest inscription.

Eternal life is defined very specifically. It is to know the one, true and living God and to honor Jesus Christ whom he sent—"God's Autobiography to the world."[3] This whole person,

2. Augustine, *Homilies on John*, 397.

3. Bruner, *John*, 967.

life-transforming, full-orbed knowing leads to everlasting joy and peace. Everlasting life means that there will be no more sin, no more sorrow, no more suffering. Scarcity and strife will cease. In Christ, evil will end. There will be a new heaven and a new earth. The healing of the nations will take place around the throne of the triune God. There will be no more night, because the Lord God will be our light. No more loneliness because the fully restoration of face-to-face fellowship with God will take place. We will no longer feel the need to hide from God.[4] No more curse means that whatever we do, "whether in word or deed, [we will] do it all in the name of the Lord Jesus, giving thanks to God the Father through him" (Col 3:17). Skeptics may say this is way too good to be true, but this is the goodness we were made for. This is the home we yearn for. C. S. Lewis observed: "We are very shy nowadays of even mentioning heaven. We are afraid of the jeer about 'pie in the sky,' and of being told that we are trying to 'escape' from the duty of making a happy world here and now into the dreams of a happy world elsewhere. But either there is a 'pie in the sky' or there is not. If there is not, then Christianity is false, for this doctrine is woven into its whole fabric. If there is, then this truth, like any other, must be faced, whether it is useful. . . . or not. Again, we are afraid that heaven is a bribe . . . "[5]

Jesus' prayer of consecration is a model for our own prayer of consecration. As he prayed for himself, we pray for ourselves: "Glorify your servant, that your servant may glorify you." If we pray this way we will soon lose our shyness about heaven and begin to live in the present in the light and life of our future home. To embrace this destiny is to experience eternal life, knowing the only true God and Jesus Christ whom he sent.

---

4. Genesis 3:8.

5. Lewis, *The Problem of Pain*, 145.

Reflections on the Way

Describe your understanding of "glory days."

What makes the cross of Jesus glorious?

Compare Jesus' understanding of glory with modern conceptions of glory.

How can we embrace the promise of heaven today?

God's Autobiography

"I have revealed your name . . ." John 17:6a

Having prayed for himself and for the perfect weekend to accomplish the Father's will perfectly, Jesus turns his intercessory attention to his disciples. Each phrase in this prayer opens up vistas of meaning that call for insight and interpretation. The Holy Spirit inspired the Scriptures to be written and read that way. You often hear scholars and preachers say that the text was designed to be unpacked, which is true enough, but the metaphor of "unpacking" seems prosaic and mechanical. The austere prose and simple cadence of Jesus prayer challenges the praying imagination of both the poet and the theologian and all of us in-between.

Jesus is God's autobiography to the world.[1] The only God to be known is the one true and living God revealed in Jesus Christ. God's very own self-representation is manifest through incarnation, mission, passion, ascension, intercession, and the coming consummation. When Jesus says, "I have revealed your name," he echoes his previous line, "I have glorified you" (John 17:4). Jesus has made God visible, his message clear, and his name known. We are more than mistaken, we are deluded, if we think we can know God apart from Jesus. The Bible is emphatic on this truth: "No one who denies the Son has the Father; whoever acknowledges the Son has the Father also" (1 John 2:23).

Commenting on the first line of the Apostle's Creed, "I believe in God, the Father Almighty, Creator of heaven and earth,"

---

1. Bruner, *John*, 967

Karl Barth insisted that knowing God the creator is only possible through knowing God the redeemer. Without the finished work of Jesus on the cross we really don't know God at all.

> The first article of faith in God the Father and His work is not a sort of 'forecourt' of the Gentiles, a realm in which Christians and Jews and Gentiles, believers and unbelievers are beside one another and to some extent stand together in the presence of a reality concerning which there might be some measure of agreement, in describing it as the work of God the Creator. . . . We are not nearer to believing in God the Creator, than we are to believing that Jesus Christ was conceived by the Holy Spirit and born of the Virgin Mary. . . .Only when we keep before us what the triune God has done for us in Jesus Christ can we realize what is involved in God the Creator and His work.[2]

Barth insisted that we cannot know the Creator apart from the Redeemer and Augustine insisted that there never was a time when the Son lacked the full revelation of the Father: "For whatever God the Father gave to God the Son, He gave in the act of begetting. For the Father gave those things to the Son without which He could not be the Son, in the same manner as He gave Him being itself. For how otherwise would He give any words to the Word, wherein in an ineffable way He hath spoken all things?"[3]

"*Your name*"—The *name*, repeated six times in Jesus' prayer, stands for the *personal* revelation of God, his character and his actions. The *name* sums up everything about the person and work of the triune God. It is more testimony than the whole of doctrinal tradition and more personal narrative than all the wisdom of creedal confession. It is about *who* rather than *what*. Jesus said to Philip, "Anyone who has seen me has seen the Father. . . .Believe me when I say that I am in the Father and the Father is in me. . ." (John 14:9-11).

---

2. Barth, *Dogmatics in Outline*, 50, 52.

3. Augustine, *Homilies* on *John*, 402.

The personal nature of the *name* reminds us that Jesus' legacy is not "a body of teaching preserved in a book—like the Qur'an. He does not leave behind an ideology or a program. He leaves behind a community—the Church."[4] The story—the long story—behind the *name* goes back to Exodus, when Moses asked God's name. How could Moses be God's representative to the people and not know the name of God? God said to Moses, "I Am Who I Am. This is what you are to say to the Israelites: 'I AM has sent me to you'" (Exod 3:14). By revealing himself in this way, God empowered Moses *personally* to lead the people of Israel out of Egypt. Similarly, the Son's revelation of the name, "If you really know me, you will know my Father as well," empowers Christ's disciples to be sent out on their mission.

As we have seen in our earlier meditations John draws out the significance of Jesus' "I AM" identification. No one else relates to us the way Jesus relates to us. The person of Christ is unique. "You call me 'Teacher' and 'Lord,' and rightly so, for that is what *I am*" (John 13:13). There are seven previous "I am" sayings in the Gospel of John, all of them declaring Christ to be the all-sufficient source for our salvation and the ground for our being. The "I am" reality of Jesus is absolutely critical for our self-identity.[5] To know this *name* is to truly know ourselves for the first time. For people who concentrate on their inner thoughts and feelings, it may be a shock to realize that knowing God is absolutely essential for self-understanding. Apart from knowing God we don't really know ourselves. But even then our chief objective in life is not to know ourselves. Our chief end is to know the *name*—the person—that is above every name (Phil 2:9) and like the Apostle Paul we come to the realization that it is better to be known than to know: "*Now I know in part; then I shall know fully, even as I am fully known*" (1 Cor 13:12).

4. Newbigin, *The Light Has Come*, 228.

5. "I am the bread of life" (6:35); "I am the light of the world." (8:12); "I am the gate of the sheep . . . I am the gate; whoever enters through me will be saved" (10:7,9); "I am the good shepherd." (10:11,14); "I am the resurrection and the life" (11:25); "I am the way and the truth and the life" (14:6); "I am the vine; you are the branches" (15:5).

Jesus' unique revelation of the *name* makes possible our witness to the Name. His prayer, "I have revealed your name," becomes our prayer. Like the Son, we have been entrusted with a mission. As his disciples we join our Lord and Savior in manifesting "the manifold wisdom of God" (Eph 3:10). As parents, friends, neighbors, and mentors we pray, "I have revealed your name to those whom you gave me out of the world." Not only did Jesus bring "many sons and daughters to glory" as only he could do, but "the one who makes people holy and those who are made holy are the same family" (Heb 2:10, 11). In the Spirit, our biography points to his autobiography of God. His story becomes our story. It is true, everyone has a story, but only one story redeems our story. And this is the story that we tell to the nations.

Reflections on the Way

What all is included in the *name* of God?

How can we say that Jesus is the autobiography of God?

Do you agree with Barth that we cannot know God the creator apart from knowing God the redeemer?

Do your friends and neighbors know that his story is your story?

The Father's Gift

"I have revealed your name to those whom you gave me out of the world. They were yours; you gave them to me and they have obeyed your word." John 17:6

Prayer reminds us that everything that we have that is worth having has been *given* to us by God. Jesus' glory prayer emphasizes the gracious *giving* of the Father. We have been *given* eternal life (John 17:2), the word of God (John 17:8,14), and participation in God's glory (John 17:22). We have received all of this because we have been *given* to the Son as a gift from the Father (John 17:2,6, 9, 24). The Son is the Father's gift to us and we are the Father's gift to the Son. We are in the habit of dwelling on the former and forgetting the latter. The Father could have given no greater gift than the gift of the Son: "For God so loved the world that he gave his one and only Son . . ." (John 3:16); "He who did not spare his own Son, but gave him up for us all—how will he not give us all things?" (Rom 8:32). But to receive the gift of the Son is to become the Father's gift to the Son.

All the giving belongs to God. There is no place in this giving equation for our merit and pride. Both our salvation and our sanctification are freely given by God. Neither saving faith nor serving faith depend upon our merit. We can only give what we have received. We are the Father's gift to the Son because we have received the Father's gift of the Son.

Parents believe that their children are a gift from God, but is there any gift more demanding than children? Yet, what is expected of loving parents is strangely (mysteriously) proportionate to the gift received. But no calculation could ever be devised to prove the logic of love's equation. Parents give and give, yet receive their children as a gift.

Marriage works in a similar way. Love receives the gift of the other with deep gratitude and joy, so that even sacrificial giving for the sake of the other is perceived as a gift gladly given. The gift of the other makes the sacrifice worth giving no matter what the cost. Parents give everything to their children, including teaching them how to give.

Perhaps these analogies help us to comprehend the gift of the Son and the giving ourselves to the Son. As the "sons and daughters of glory" we have been given a gift greater than the gift of a child or the gift of a spouse. The incomparable gift of the Son is the greatest gift we can imagine. To receive the Father's gift of the Son is to be inspired and empowered by God's Holy Spirit to be the Father's gift to the Son. This is how we learn to value the gift of the Son; we become the Father's gift to the Son. The old giving-getting contract of works righteousness is swept aside, replaced by the gracious giving of the Father. We say with the Apostle Paul, "whatever were gains to me I now consider loss for the sake of Christ" (Phil 3:7).

One of Jesus' parables comes to mind. His no-big-deal-work-ethic parable underscores the covenant of grace (Luke 17:7-10). Faithful disciples can never put God in their debt. We are not accruing credit through our faithful service, we are simply doing what God's grace has gifted and empowered us to do. Jesus told the story this way: "Suppose one of you has a servant plowing or looking after his sheep. Will he say to the servant when he comes in from the field, 'Come along now and sit down to eat'? Won't he rather say, 'Prepare my supper, get yourself ready and wait on me while I eat and drink; after that you may eat and drink'? Will he thank the servant because he did what he was told to do? So you also, when you have done everything you were told to do, should say, 'We are unworthy servants; we have only done our duty.'"

We are the privileged recipients of both sides of the Father's giving. We are the gift because we have received the gift. We neither earn our place in the family of God nor take credit for our role in the family. This is why Jesus said in the upper room, "I no longer call you servants, because servants do not know their master's business. Instead, I have called you friends, for everything that I learned from my Father I have made known to you. You did not choose me, but I chose you and appointed you so that you might go and bear fruit—fruit that will last"(John 15:15-16).

Reflections on the Way

Have you ever thought of yourself as the Father's gift to the Son?

How do the analogies of parenting and marriage lead us into a deeper understanding of God's strategy of giving?

What does it mean for us to be always on the receiving end?

How does all this divine giving inspire and empower our giving?

Other-Worldly Followers

"I have revealed your name to those whom you
gave me out of the world. They were yours; you
gave them to me and they have obeyed your
word." John 17:6

Disciples are described in two ways. They are "out of the
world" and obedient to the word. These two aspects, otherworldliness and obedience, focus on the same reality—the same
identity—from two different angles. Jesus' prayer cites an accomplishment not an aspiration. This is who we are, otherworldly
obedient disciples. Jesus said, "You *are* the salt of the earth . . . You
are the light of the world," *not* you will be (Matt 5:13-14). He underscores the cause and effect of true discipleship as a "given" in
the life of the disciples. Obedience to his word is the cause; otherworldliness is the effect. This description is true of all believers.
There is no elite band of *obedient* disciples and another group of
ordinary *worldly* Christians.

We cannot pick and choose what we want to obey, anymore
than a Navy Seal can decide which orders he wants to obey and
which ones he wants to ignore. We are all under one Lord and Savior, Jesus Christ. At times the church has distinguished between
the counsels of perfection and ordinary commands, but Jesus and
the apostles resisted any notion of elitism. Jesus never envisioned
a two- or three-tiered hierarchy of spirituality, nor a clergy-laity
division, much less the meaningless distinction between "true believers" and "average churchgoers."

We want to be followers of Jesus—abiding in Christ, not just religious admirers. Every believer is meant to be a disciple, every disciple a believer. There are no *almost* Christians in the New Testament. Jesus and the apostles kept the distinction clear. But it seems easy today to blur the distinction and make ourselves out to be followers, when in effect we are only worldly admirers of Jesus. Admirers are neither obedient nor otherworldly. They look on Jesus as a success symbol or an icon for living, but admirers don't imitate his life or obey his word.

Admirers seem to assume that they already know what they need to know about Jesus. Religious familiarity obscures the meaning of true spirituality. Instead of the crucified Lord, who calls us to take up our cross and follow him, they imagine Jesus blessing their vision of success. But sadly an almost Christian is not an altogether Christian.

The Danish Christian thinker Søren Kierkegaard believed that the life of Jesus "from beginning to end, was calculated only to procure *followers*, and calculated to make *admirers* impossible."[1]

> His life was *the Truth*, which constitutes precisely the re-
> lationship in which admiration is untruth . . . But when
> *the truth*, true to itself in being the truth, little by little,
> more and more definitely, unfolds itself as the truth, the
> moment comes when no admirer can hold out with it,
> a moment when it shakes admirers from it as the storm
> shakes the worm-eaten fruit from the tree.[2]

Kierkegaard reasoned that the desire to admire instead of obey was not the invention of bad people; "no, it is the flabby invention of what one may call the better sort of [people], but weak people for all that, in their effort to hold themselves aloof."[3] Instead of working out their salvation with fear and trembling, admirers choose the features of Christianity that they like best, such as inspirational services and felt-need programs. Out of fear of being otherworldly

1. Kierkegaard, *Training in Christianity*, 232.
2. Ibid., 239.
3. Ibid., 237.

successful churches cater to admiration over obedience to attract large numbers of admirers.

To be "kept in the holy name of God" requires commitments to be made that lie "outside the comprehension of the world."[4] "If the Church does not rest on a point outside the world it has no leverage with the world." Missionary statesman Lesslie Newbigin continues, "The Church is marked off from the world by the fact that it has received and must witness to the word of God which is the truth and which calls in question all the so-called axioms, absolutes, and self-evident propositions which are the stock-in-trade of the world's life."[5] The transformation from worldly conformity to otherworldly obedience is "not a human possibility; it is a gift of God, a miracle, a new birth from above."[6] Conversion marks the boundary between the wisdom of the age and the wisdom of God (1 Cor 1:18-31). We used to be at home in this world, but because we have been born again "into a living hope" we are now foreigners, elect exiles, and resident aliens in our home culture (1 Pet 1:1, 3; 2:11).

This single verse in Jesus' glory prayer unites the gift of grace with the gift of service. Having received the gift we become the gift. And having been called out of the world, obedience calls us back into the world for the sake of the gospel. Otherworldliness and obedience cannot be separated. This is why there can never be two church growth strategies, one to grow the church numerically and another to grow it spiritually. Obedient otherworldliness makes it impossible to have a biblical approach to spiritual growth and a marketing approach to numerical growth. This is why worldly leadership is incompatible with biblical leadership. Those who seek to use the world's ways to fulfill God's aims have yet to wrestle with the radical discontinuity between what Jesus wants in a follower and what the world expects in an admirer.

What works for Walmart does not work for the kingdom of God. This is why the humanitarian impact of the gospel must

4. Newbigin, *The Light Has Come*, 231.
5. Ibid.
6. Ibid.

never lose sight of the gospel. Salvation is the cardinal doctrine of the gospel. Sincere believers can be "easily led off the track of leading people to salvation" by striving to improve social conditions. Humanitarian efforts are great, but "social services are never a substitute for the process of salvation." Scot McKnight warns, "When Christians get out of balance here, it is always the message of salvation that gets lost."[7]

The otherworldliness that is defined by obedience to the word of God refuses to conform the gospel to a comfortable cloister or reduce the gospel to a moralistic agenda. It resists an unbiblical separation from the world and a cultural conformity to tradition. This is the otherworldliness that loves the world by not loving the things of the world—"the lust of the flesh, the lust of the eyes and the pride of life" (1 John 2:16). This is the obedient otherworldliness that loves the world with the love of the Father who gave his one and only Son for the world.

Reflections on the Way

Do you agree that the followers of Jesus are marked by obedience and otherworldliness?

Describe the difference between a "follower" and an "admirer."

What is the impact of grace-shaped discipleship?

How can Christians love the world the way Jesus did?

---

7. McKnight, *1 Peter*, 81.

"I Gave Them The Words"

"Now they know that everything you have given me comes from you. For I gave them the words you gave me and they accepted them."
John 17:7, 8a

Jesus' intercessory prayer exudes confidence. His disciples know that his revelation of the Father is authentic and complete. Jesus is not on his own making it up as he goes. Everything he gives has been given by the Father: "Very truly I tell you, the Son can do nothing by himself" (John 5:19). Jesus is confident that the disciples have accepted the Word, not just in theory but in fact. Their acceptance translates into reverent obedience. It means that they are committed to keeping the Word and honoring the Word. They are locked into the meaning of the message of Christ. The Apostle Paul will spell out what this acceptance means when he writes, "Let the word of Christ dwell in you richly as you teach and admonish one another with all wisdom. . . . And whatever you do, whether in word or deed, do it all in the name of the Lord Jesus, giving thanks to God the Father through him" (Col 3:16-17).

If this is what "knowing" and "accepting" means, were the disciples truly worthy of Jesus' confidence? Judging from the immediate context, Augustine said, "No." The disciples did not yet have the character to believe and obey "without constraint, with firmness, constancy, and fortitude."[1] They were after all about to cut and run and leave Jesus alone. Augustine reasoned that Jesus

1. Augustine, *Homilies on John*, 401.

was "declaring beforehand what sort they were yet to be" when they had "received the Holy Spirit, who, according to the promise, should teach them all things."[2] Augustine contended that Jesus' prophetic confidence, spoken in the past tense, was based on the fact that the disciples had not yet moved from their pre-passion doubt and timidity to their post-passion devotion and boldness.

But what if instead of comparing the disciples before and after passion and Pentecost we compare the disciples' receptivity to the Word and the world's rejection of the Word before the passion? If we place the disciples "in the stream of redemptive history" their belief and obedience before the resurrection stands out in comparison to the unbelief and disobedience of the world. No matter how "flawed their courage might have been" they boldly declared their loyalty to Jesus, "You have the words of eternal life and we have come to believe that you are the Holy One of God" (John 6:68-69).[3]

Regardless of how we frame the disciples' belief, Jesus' confidence lies not so much in his disciples as it does in the Spirit of God. When Peter confessed, "You are the Christ, the Son of the living God," Jesus replied, "Blessed are you, Simon son of Jonah, for this was not revealed to you by flesh and blood, but by my Father in heaven" (Matt 16:16-17). We remain flawed, fearful, and frail disciples even after true conversion and the gift of the Holy Spirit, nevertheless Jesus' prayed out confidence remains valid because it depends on the Spirit of God and the Word of God.

Jesus' prophetic confidence was in the *first* disciples with whom he was praying. In that circle on that fateful night, Jesus honored "their specific fidelity." They had "kept" the Father's Word. Dale Bruner continues, "We can trust that what the apostles gave us in their writings is nothing more nor less than the words of Jesus . . . the very Word of God himself. This is no little fidelity. It amounts to a claim of inspiration."[4]

2. Ibid.
3. Carson, *John*, 559.
4. Bruner, *John*, 984.

Our confidence today is not in ourselves but in Christ and his Word. A story that helps illustrate this is Cormac McCarthy's *The Sunset Limited*. The one-act play is a conversation between a Black man and White man which takes place in a tenement building in a black ghetto in New York City. In the movie version, Samuel Lee Jackson brings the white professor played by Tommy Lee Jones back to his apartment after rescuing him from an attempted suicide. Black tries to convince White that life is worth living, because he wants assurance that White won't throw himself in front of a train again. The ensuing conversation is a brilliant back and forth point-counterpoint between an ex-con who has found real hope in Christ and a professor who has given up on life. Black's simple faith is in dialogue with White's sophisticated nihilism. In the end, White says, "I'm sorry. You're a kind man, but I have to go. I've heard you out and you've heard me and there's no more to say. Your God must have once stood in a dawn of infinite possibility and this is what he's made of it. And now it is drawing to a close. You say that I want God's love. I don't. Perhaps I want forgiveness, but there is no one to ask it of. And there is no going back. No setting things right. Perhaps once. Not now. Now there is only the hope of nothingness. I cling to that hope. Now open the door. Please."[5]

Black reluctantly undoes the bolts, opens the door and the professor exits. Black collapses to his knees, all but weeping. He feels utterly defeated in his attempt to rescue White and convince him of the hope he has in Christ. In desperation, he looks up, and cries out to God, "He didn't mean them words. You know he didn't."

And then he says something that recalls Peter's exhortation "to always be prepared to give an answer . . . for the hope you have." Black says, "I don't understand what you sent me down there for. I don't understand it. If you wanted me to help him how come you didn't give me the words? You give 'em to him. What about me?" Black kneels, weeping back and forth. Then, he says, "That's all right. That's all right. If you never speak again you know I'll keep

5. McCarthy, *The Sunset Limited*, 141.

your word. You know I will. You know I'm good for it." He lifts his head. "Is that okay? Is that okay?"

Black's sense of inadequacy and apparent inability to meet the professor's intellectual arguments are feelings commonly shared by Christians who share the first disciples confidence in the Word of God. We feel Black's deep sense of defeat, even despair at our inability to convince the world of our hope in Christ. We ask along with him, why doesn't God give us just the right words to knock down the nihilist's arguments or the hedonist's philosophy or the religionist's system? But we are not looking for a bullet-proof apologetic. The challenge is not to have all the right words, but to keep the Word. Black acquired this insight painfully, but expressed it beautifully, when he says to God, "If you never speak again you know I'll keep your word."[6]

Reflections on the Way

How do you compare yourself to these first disciples?

Unlike the world around them, the disciples were responsive to Jesus' word. How is their response to Jesus a model for us?

Is your confidence in the word of God growing?

What is the difference between finding the right words and keeping the word?

6. Ibid., 142.

Certainty

> "Now they know *that* everything you have given
> me comes from you. For I gave them the words
> you gave me and they accepted them. They knew
> with certainty *that* I came from you, and they
> believed *that* you sent me." John 17:7-8

Jesus is confident. On the eve of his crucifixion, Jesus' prayer expresses a settled confidence not only in his finished work but in the certainty of the disciples' conviction. This is the kind of report that receives the Father's commendation, "Well done, good and faithful servant, enter into the joy of your reward." Only in his case, it is the Son not the servant that has successfully completed the Father's work. Jesus measures the success of his mission by the certainty of the disciples. Because they knew with certainty that Jesus' every act, his every word, and his very being were from the Father, they believed that he was sent by the Father and was one with the Father. "Jesus in every important respect is the direct derivative of God the Father and not just a great or deeply spiritual man."[1] The joy of being able to pray this way before the cross must have been deeply encouraging to Jesus. The Christ-centered certainty of the first disciples forms the foundation for the faith of all Christ's followers. This is the certainty that calms our anxiety; the clarity that cuts through our confusion.

The New Testament epistles thrive on this certainty. There is nothing vague or tentative about the early church's confident

1. Bruner, *John*, 985.

certainty in Christ. Hebrews begins by declaring boldly that true spirituality is not found in a vague, undefined emotive feeling that stirs the self. True spirituality is not to be confused with soul-inspiring music or incredible sports plays or altruistic acts of human kindness. These are all wonderful, but true spirituality is found in the specific revelation of God found in Jesus Christ.

Vague notions of Christ formed in our imagination are dismissed in favor of the Son who is "the exact representation" of the Father. Confidence is placed in the one who "is the very image of the essence of God—the impress of his being." The Son is the "perfect imprint of the very being of God."[2] "What God essentially is, is made manifest in Christ. To see Christ is to see what the Father is like."[3] There is no generic, nameless, pre-Christian deity to be known. Only God the Father, Son, and Holy Spirit can be known and only the Son reveals the very being of God.

This is why we exegete the Gospels, because they exegete the life of Jesus. This why we expound the epistles, because of the truth that is in Jesus (Eph 4:21). This is the bold truth celebrated throughout the Bible. The Apostle John writes, "That which was from the beginning, which we have heard, which we have seen with our eyes, which we have looked at and our hands have touched—this we proclaim concerning the Word of life" (1 John 1:1-2).

Commenting on the difference between gospel-centered clarity and cultural Christianity, missiologist Timothy Tennent writes, "When you walk into a vibrant church, you can immediately sense the difference. At every point, you meet gospel clarity. The church exudes confidence in the unique work of Jesus Christ. They understand the power and authority of God's Word. They feel the lostness of the world and the urgency to bring the good news to everyone. At every point, you observe gospel clarity. . . .The clarity is palatable. It is infectious. You can actually sense the presence of Christ in your midst."

2. Cockerill, *Hebrews*, 94.

3. Bruce, *Hebrews*, 48.

Tennent continues, "In contrast, when you walk into the churches in decline you are immediately brought into 'the Fog.' What is the fog? It is the inability to be clear about anything. There is no clarity about who Jesus Christ is and what He has done. There is no clarity about the Scriptures as the authoritative Word of God. There is no clarity about the urgency to reach the lost. . . . In the 'fog,' Jesus Christ is just one of many noble teachers in the world."[4]

Jesus' confidence in the first disciples certainty is a challenge to contemporary believers. He believed in his original band because they believed in him. Their four-fold confidence in Jesus' acts, words, being, and mission depended directly on the Father and was meant to be embraced confidently by today's believers— by you and me. Apostolic Christology needs to be our Christology! At the outset of his ministry, when the people were impressed by his signs, John reports that "Jesus would not entrust himself to them, for he knew all people" (John 2:24). Now, in his final prayer with his disciples before the cross Jesus revels in the believing certainty of his disciples' faith in him.

Reflections on the Way

Does Jesus believe in you and pray for you the way he prayed for the first disciples?

How do you account for the bold Christ-centered explicitness of the New Testament epistles?

How is gospel clarity tied to church vitality?

Does the world around us observe our pre-passion doubt and confusion or our post-resurrection confidence and certainty?

4. Tennent, "Gospel Clarity vs. 'The Fog.'"

DAY 22

Strategic Refusal

"I pray for them. I am not praying for the world,
but for those you have given me, for they are
yours. All I have is yours, and all you have is mine.
And the glory has come to me through them."

John 17:9-10

Jesus prays for himself and for his disciples. He knows better than anyone else that this is the only way to help the world. Jesus and his disciples are not of this world but they are *for* the world. The world is very much on the mind of Jesus. He references the "world" fifteen times in his prayer! And in a moment Jesus will be praying dearly for the world, "so that the world may believe that you have sent me," but for now he prays for the disciples. He does not pray for the world.

Jesus refuses to pray for the world for a strategic reason. It is not because he does not love the world. Even the youngest believer knows that. It is because his first disciples come first in bringing salvation to the world. "The original apostolic disciples are the Father's most special missionary gift to his Son."[1] Jesus keeps emphasizing that the disciples are a gift from the Father. To paraphrase Jesus on this *gift*: "You gave them to me out of the world. You gave them to me and they have obeyed your word. You gave them your word through me. You gave them me and they know I am yours."

1. Bruner, *John*, 987.

Jesus is not *preaching* to his disciples in his *prayer* (as some pastors do in their prayers) but he is expressing his deep gratitude for the gift of the disciples, because they are absolutely critical for saving the world. As strange as it may seem to the world, this called-out community of apostolic disciples is the means chosen by God to reach the world with the gospel. This "motley little Galilean crew," to quote Bruner, is "the most important and salvific community on the planet."[2] Jesus prayed that the apostolic disciples and all those disciples who follow in their steps would see themselves in this radically other-worldly way. There is plenty of room for God's common grace to be expressed in all manner of humanitarian effort, but Jesus prays here for the specific manifestation of his saving grace through the apostolic community. The Trinitarian symmetry of Jesus' "equality of honor,"[3] "All I have is yours, and all you have is mine," makes it all the more remarkable that Jesus prayed, "And glory has come to me through them." God has chosen to measure his glory through the mission of this "motley little Galilean crew" who as we know will turn the world upside down (Acts 17:6).

There is no point in praying for the world if the priority of the gospel is not kept primary. The prophet Jeremiah provides an provocative precedent for Jesus' strategic refusal. The Lord told Jeremiah three times not to pray for "this people." Jeremiah came at the end of a long line of prophets who had pled with the people to repent and turn to the Lord. The people's refusal led the Lord to say to Jeremiah, "Do not plead with me, for I will not listen to you" (Jer 7:16). Spirituality, apart from the will of God, is always an exercise in futility. The religious enthusiasm, rhetoric, and ritual in Jeremiah's day counted for nothing because it was void of true faith and faithfulness. Yahweh commanded, "Do not pray. . . . because I will not listen when they call to me in the time of distress" (Jer 11:14). To hide the gospel, whether in Jeremiah's day or in our own and ingratiate ourselves to the world through prayer will always be a big mistake. The Lord was adamant, "Do not pray for

2. Ibid.

3. Chrysostom, *Homilies on John*, 300

the well-being of this people. Although they fast, I will not listen to their cry . . ." (Jer 14:11).

Jesus' prayer is paradoxical. It teaches disciples not to pray for the world in worldly ways. If we use prayer as a worldly religious tool to assuage the world's grief without receiving the Father's gift of the Son, we undercut the apostolic witness. If we use cut-flower prayers to sentimentalize and spiritualize our relationship to the world, the world will be more than happy to grant the church a ceremonial presence. But I doubt that The Lord's Lord's Prayer would have gone over well at a Presidential Prayer Breakfast.

Jesus' simple statement, "I pray for them," coupled with, "for they are yours," underscores the familial bond Jesus felt with the Father on behalf of the disciples. Their shared life together made Jesus intercessory prayer a family prayer. It is fitting that he should pray for the "sons and daughters" he is bringing to glory (Heb 2:10). Loving parents who value the love of their children can understand what Jesus means when he prays, "And glory has come to me through them." There is a kind of relational pride that leads to heartfelt prayer.

Reflections on the Way

Why does Jesus say that he is not praying for the world?

How is this a "strategic refusal"?

What do his prayed-for disciples have that the world doesn't have and needs?

How should we pray for the world?

Protected

> "I will remain in the world no longer, but they are still in the world, and I am coming to you. Holy Father, protect them by the power of your name, the name you gave me, so that they may be one as we are one." John 17:11

Since Jesus didn't change the world, his disciples need not try. Jesus' strategic refusal to pray for the world is linked to his sober analysis of the disciples' place in the world. In the absence of his limited earth-bound self from the world, Jesus promised greater works, but the greater works did not include changing the world. The greater works have to do with the global scope of the gospel, the power of sacrificial love, the enduring comfort of the Holy Spirit, and the hope of resilient saints who against all odds establish a faithful presence in a hostile world. These are the greater works that belong to the eschatological fulfillment of the gospel, not to our wish dreams and our entrepreneurial visions. When Jesus says, "You may ask me for anything in my name, and I will do it" (John 15:13), our minds are tempted to fly off in a million directions. We want to lift the promise out of the context of Jesus' life and ministry and forget the challenge to take up our cross daily and follow Jesus.

To hear Jesus' intercessory prayer is to scrutinize our naive notions of the world. The idea that the world will change if we change enough "hearts and minds" and "get out the vote" underestimates the complex and systemic nature of evil. Many Christians who think that they are "on fire for Jesus" have no idea how deeply they are conformed to this world. We may see ourselves as world-changers but in reality we are products of the world. Even transformed "hearts and minds" are naive in the face of cultural conformity and capitulation. This is why the idolatry of money, sports, sex, and selfish pleasure is such a problem among professing Christians.

Judging from the Apostle Peter's New Testament epistle he heard Jesus' prayer with both ears and a keen mind. Peter was never given a vision of heroic service, only the longsuffering, persevering, pastoral care responsibilities required of the shepherd. Jesus did not call Peter, "To change the world," or "Lead an army," or "Launch a crusade," or "Compete with Rome." Jesus didn't even say, "Build my kingdom." He said, "Feed my sheep." Peter and the apostles "turned the world upside down," but they didn't change the world. It never occurred to them to do so and nowhere in the New Testament is there any hint that they intended to.

In the Spirit, Peter developed an altogether different vision of Jesus Christ and the Christian's calling than the one often popularized in our culture. For Peter, Jesus is the obedient one whose sacrificial death secures salvation for all those born again into a living hope. Peter's emphasis is on the inheritance to come, the believer's eschatological hope, and the culmination of our salvation when Christ comes again. On this side of eternity he envisions a sacrificial life of holy obedience, rather than the fulfillment of the American dream, personal success, and the material good life.

Peter challenged the people of God to accept the gospel's revolutionary strategy. He urged them to embrace their "foreign" status and to see themselves as "elect exiles," "chosen outsiders," and "resident aliens." Their new birth into a "living hope," into "an inheritance that can never perish, spoil or fade" spared Christians the fear and resentment intrinsic to worldly conformity and competition. Peter envisioned chosen outsiders "filled with an inexpressible and glorious joy."

Jesus prayed to the *Holy Father* for protection. This is the only time in the Gospel of John that Jesus addressed the Father in a way that combines "awesome transcendence with familial intimacy."[1]

---

1. Carson, *John*, 561; Beasley-Murray, *John*, 299.

The accent on *holiness* emphasizes "separation from the profane world" and underscores the "burden of the prayer" as "deliverance from the evil power of the world."[2] "The Father is asked to grant to the disciples his own immunity from evil."[3] Jesus' sober assessment of the world leads him to pray for protection and sanctification. Missing in his prayer is any hint of making the world a better place.

Jesus intercessory prayer challenges the triumphal dreaming and guilt-inducing blame that claims the world is as bad as it is because Christians have failed to grasp the reins of power. The world is the world and the world will be the world until Christ comes again. "The world can be prayed for only to the end that some who now belong to it might abandon it and join with others who have been chosen out of the world."[4] Jesus is not calling Christians to aspire for cultural greatness or join the ranks of the elite or and take back America in a groundswell of populist support. Jesus' humble prayer for protection is humiliating to the misguided soul who seeks to impose his or her worldly vision on the church and turn the gospel into a great crusade or a grand cause. Jesus did not set his sights too low; he set his sights on the Holy Father.

Reflections on the Way

If our mission is not to grab the reins of power, what is our mission?

In what ways are Christians tempted to become a product of the world?

How are we protected in the world from the world by the Holy Father?

What does it mean for you to be a faithful presence for Christ in the world?

2. Temple, *Readings in St. John's Gospel*, 318.

3. Ibid.

4. Carson, *John*, 561.

DAY 24

Power in the Name

"Holy Father, protect them by the power of your
name, the name you gave me, so that they may be
one as we are one." John 17:11

When we adopted our two sons as infants they received a new name—our name. Confidentiality prevented us from knowing their previous surnames but that didn't much matter to us. We were so excited to adopt them into our family. Out of deep gratitude and the providence of God Jeremiah and Andrew were chosen to be in our family, chosen to be loved, nurtured, and protected in our little household of faith. When their sister was conceived naturally, it only underscored for us that there was little difference in the bond of love between biological conception and adoption.

Their adoption serves as a redemptive analogy for me, making my own adoption in Christ and the language Paul used to describe adoption more vivid. "For he chose us in him before the creation of the world to be holy and blameless in his sight. In love he predestined us for adoption to sonship through Jesus Christ ..." (Eph 1:4-5). In Christ we are given a new name and a radically new identity.

Although our sons look like they could be our biological offspring and our parental nurture has played a role in their personal development, their natural gifts and personalities definitely demonstrate our family's expanded gene pool. They couldn't help but bring a rich diversity of aptitudes and talents into our family.

Not only are they very different from each other, they are very different from their parents. But this diversity is both challenging and enriching. It has only served to strengthen our family unity and deepen our affection for one another. This too, is a redemptive analogy for me, because the family of God, the body of Christ, the apostolic community, is a richly diversified church, drawn from "every tribe and language and people and nation" (Rev 5:9).

Jesus prayed, "Holy Father, protect them by the power of your name, the name you gave me, so that they may be one as we are one." Jesus wants the Trinitarian oneness, the essential unity between the Father, the Son, and the Holy Spirit, to characterize the entire church. He introduces the *one* church theme here so we will "hear it as an increasingly steady drumbeat in the concluding sentences of his prayer."[1] The key to this unity abides in the power of the name, which represents the fullness of God's character, that is, the whole revealed reality of God. The first disciples knew that Christ's purpose "was to create in himself one new humanity" (Eph 2:15). The racial, gender, generational, social, and economic divides were meant to be overcome in Christ. "There is neither Jew nor Gentile, neither slave nor free, neither male nor female, for you are all one in Christ Jesus" (Gal 3:28).

Believers in northern Ghana may understand their new tribe identity more easily than western believers. Conversion and baptism bring immediate clarity and solidarity. In a village in northern Ghana, steeped in ancient animism and rituals, a believer's commitment to Jesus Christ cannot be kept secret. Overnight Christ's followers become, in Peter's words, "chosen outsiders," "elect exiles," and "resident aliens" (1 Pet 1:1, 17; 2:11). Western believers struggle with this new tribe identity. We are steeped in individualism and personal autonomy. We see ourselves as little chiefs with multiple tribal identities: family, school, work, sports, hobbies, church, friends, and entertainment. We are over-committed, over-worked, and over-busy. Church is one small compartment in a highly competitive environment. Our multiple tribal identities, each with its own set of cultural customs, rituals, offerings, and

---

1. Bruner, *John*, 989.

obligations, compete for our loyalty. Colleagues at work, next-door neighbors, work-out friends, and even family members may not even know we belong to the new tribe.

To know this name is not a matter of head-knowledge, but of whole person, heartfelt, life-transforming commitment. We associate this kind of knowing with deep friendship or marriage. I often conclude a wedding meditation by saying, "A man leaves his father and mother to be united to his wife. He offers a name, she receives a name. The two are united under a new name. This is great but there is another name I want you to think about. Another name more powerful and more enduring that you want to be known by, "And whatever you do, whether in word or deed, do it all in the name of the Lord Jesus Christ, giving thanks to God the Father through him" (Col 3:17).

Reflections on the Way

How have you experienced this new family identity in Christ?

In what ways have you experienced the fullness of the family of God?

How are we protected and unified by the name of the Holy Father?

Do people in your world know about your "new tribe" identity?

DAY 25

Safe-Keeping

"While I was with them, I protected them and
kept them safe by that name you gave me. None
has been lost except the one doomed to destruction so that Scripture would be fulfilled."
John 17:11-12

We are kept by the power of the name in the same way Jesus
protected the first disciples. Not surprisingly the two "pro-
tections" run in marked continuity: like Father, like Son. By drawing this connection Jesus takes the secrecy out of faithfulness. The
challenge remains the same for today's disciples as it was for the
first disciples. Jesus said, "If you hold to my teaching, you are really
my disciples. Then you will know the truth, and the truth will set
you free" (John 8:31-32).

The *keeping* power of the gospel is found in faithfulness to the
Word of God and in the abiding real presence of Christ. Among
the first disciples, Judas was the exception that proved the rule.
"None" were lost, but "the one doomed to destruction." Jesus in-
dicated in the upper room that Judas' defection was no surprise.
Jesus used the Psalms to process the unnatural betrayal of "the son
of perdition": "Even my close friend, someone I trusted, one who
shared my bread, has turned against me" (Ps 41:9). Judas stands
as a sober warning to all of Christ's followers, but we should note
that his example doesn't make betrayal look easy. On the contrary,
Judas makes defection look incredibly foolish, extremely difficult,
and painfully self-destructive.

Wang Mangdao, affectionately known as the "Dean of the House Churches" in China, resisted being co-opted by the Chinese Communist government in much the same way that Dietrich Bonhoeffer resisted the "ideology and theology that sanctioned Nazi suppression of Christian dissent."[1] From 1924 to 1955 Wang Mangdao was a powerful advocate for evangelical Christianity. He stressed repentance, conversion and sanctification (moral purity). He shunned institutional and political entanglements and refused to join the Three-Self Patriotic Movement (Self-government, Self-support, and Self-propagation). He saw the Three-Self Church (TSPM) as a cover for Communist Party control and a capitulation to liberal modernism (the Social Gospel) resulting in the ideological captivity of the church. He reasoned that it was absolutely vital to keep a distinction between true followers of Jesus Christ and unbelievers.

On August 7, 1955 Wang preached a sermon entitled, "This Is How They Betrayed the Son of Man" to some seven to eight hundred worshipers. Late that night he, along with his wife Jingwen, was arrested at gunpoint. For the next twelve months Wang was subject to daily harassment, deprivations, accusations, and threats. His interrogators broke him physically, psychologically, and spiritually. On September 30, 1956, Wang delivered his forced confession before a crowd of TSPM religious leaders. He along with his wife were released the next day and allowed to return to the parsonage. His biographer Thomas Harvey describes Wang Mingdao's state of mind: "Wang Mindao's torment, however, continued. Shaken by the confession, Wang hardly spoke. . . . Haunted by the events of the last year, Wang was thought by some to have suffered a nervous breakdown. He was overheard crying out that he was 'Judas' and observed behaving erratically. Jingwen feared that he might take his life, as his father had, should his despair grow too great . . ."[2]

Wang still could not bring himself to join the TSPM and after seven months he was rearrested and sentenced to fifteen years of

1. Harvey, *Acquainted with Grief*, 9.
2. Ibid., 99.

hard labor which was later extended to life imprisonment. It was never Wang's concern to overthrow the government or resist the state. His concern was entirely focused on maintaining an authentic Christian testimony, doctrinal integrity, moral purity, and upholding the authority of God's Word, the Bible. It was never about communism vs. capitalism or socialism vs. democracy. For Wang Mingdao it was always about Christ and his church.

Wang Mingdao might have died in prison if the Spirit of God had not helped him come to terms with the humiliation of his forced confession. In 1963 on verge of complete physical exhaustion and emotional despair he came upon a passage of Scripture that brought him great hope: "But as for me, I will look to the Lord, I will wait for the God of my salvation; my God will hear me. Do not rejoice over me, O my enemy; when I fall, I shall rise; when I sit in darkness, the Lord will be a light to me. I must bear the indignation of the Lord, because I have sinned against him" (Mic 7:7-9a).

"Flooded with a peace that overwhelmed his dark night of incarceration," Harvey writes, "he felt released to live out a radical liberation."[3] Even though Wang Mingdao remained imprisoned for another sixteen years he became a resilient saint. He came to see himself more like Peter than Judas. In the end he had *not* fallen away; in a moment of pressure and persecution he had only scattered.

Reflections on the Way

How is your faithfulness to Christ challenged?

What are the best ways to protect your faith?

How do you respond to Wang Mingdao's story?

Is Jesus' prayer for our protection reflected in our resilience?

3. Ibid., 116.

DAY 26

Enemy Talk

"I am coming to you now, but I say these things
while I am still in the world, so that they may have
the full measure of my joy within them. I have
given them your word and the world has hated
them, for they are not of the world any more than
I am of the world." John 17:13-14

We are reminded of the thin line between devotion and dialogue. Jesus' moves easily from communion with the Father
to conversation with his disciples. Jesus is praying with and for the
disciples. He prays to the Holy Father for his own sake and for the
sake of his first disciples, and he prays not only for them, but for all
of us who follow in their steps. Jesus has already covered joy and
hate in his discipleship sermon (John 15:11,18), now he sees fit to
pray through these important themes. For Jesus there is only a thin
line between prayer and preaching, preaching and prayer.

The striking juxtaposition of complete joy and the world's
hate assumes that the disciple's joy and peace does not rest on
worldly circumstances. Resilient saints take heart! In the world
you will have trouble—plenty of trouble, but Jesus has overcome
the world (John 16:33). Jesus distinguishes his joy from every
other form of worldly happiness with the simplest of all possessive
pronouns, "my." This is the joy that is as far removed from our own
self-efforts at happiness as we can imagine. There is no room in this
joy for a private, individualized, spiritualized religious experience
that lets *me* focus on *my* self and *my* religious tastes and spiritual

preferences. We cannot manufacture or give ourselves this joy; it is the gift of God.

This is the joy unperturbed by Jesus' warning: "Do not suppose that I have come to bring peace to the earth. I did not come to bring peace, but a sword" (Matt 10:34), prompting Oswald Chambers to write, "Jesus Christ came to 'bring . . . a sword' through every kind of peace that is not based on a personal relationship with Himself."[1] And John Calvin to say, "Peace with God is contrasted with every form of intoxicated security in the flesh."[2] This is the distinctive joy that is consistent with the high cost of discipleship and Jesus' invitation, "If anyone would come after me, he must deny himself and take up his cross daily and follow me. For whoever wants to save his life will lose it, but whoever loses his life for me will save it" (Luke 9:23-24).

Sadly, this is the joy that provokes the world's hate. William Temple wrote, "The world hates anything which it cannot understand which yet seems to contain a judgment of itself."[3] John Chrysostom chalked it up to "the natural course of things," because Christian virtue "engenders hatred." "Let us not grieve," Chrysostom wrote, "for this is a mark of virtue." This is why Christ said, "If you were of the world, the world would love its own."[4] Dale Bruner's reflection on the world's hate is especially helpful. The world's hate for the Word and the Church is "a great mystery" stemming from the fact that believers are rooted "in Jesus, his Father, the Paraclete Spirit, the Church, Holy Scripture, the major creeds, and world mission." The world finds these roots provocative and translates each one into something to be despised: "an otherworldly Teacher, an unreal God, a specious Spirit, a hypocritical Church, a misleading Scripture, dogmatic creeds, and an arrogant mission."[5]

---

1. Oswald Chambers, *My Utmost for His Highest*, Dec. 19.
2. Quoted in Barth, *Dogmatics in Outline*, 151.
3. Temple, *Readings in St. John's Gospel*, 322.
4. Chrysostom, *Homilies on John*, 302.
5. Bruner, *John*, 991.

Prayerful recognition of evil is the first step in dealing with the enemy. Jesus does not conceal the fact that the gospel draws enemy fire. By naming the enemy, Jesus lays bare the harsh realities confronting the people of God. The example of his real prayer is an antidote to boring, placid prayers. All this enemy talk triggers our adrenaline. We are in a spiritual combat zone, but we are not alone and we are under orders. Our deep concern and prayer should be that it is truly the Word of God that draws enemy fire and not any of our obnoxious and offensive ways. We have not been called of God to flee the world or fight the world. Nor have we been called to withdraw into our own tight-knit enclaves. We were never meant to impress the world as narrow-minded, opinionated separatists. The offense of the cross ought to be the most winsome and attractive "offensiveness" that human culture has ever known.

There is no excuse for Jesus' disciples to be filled with fear and anger and resentment; and certainly no reason to meet insult with insult and slander with slander. We are to be like Joseph in Pharaoh's Egypt and Daniel in Nebuchadnezzar's Babylon. This is what it means to be salt and light in a fallen world. The world has nothing to fear from Christians other than the demonstration of God's goodness. We will not fight the world with the weapons of the world. Like Jesus, we are marked by the cross. The Apostle Peter followed his master's example. His aim, as well as ours, ought to be to encourage believers as "foreigners and exiles" to "live such good lives among the pagans" that the world may see the goodness of God "and glorify God on the day he visits us" (1 Pet 2:12).

Reflections on the Way

How have you experienced this juxtaposition of joy and hate?

In what ways has Jesus Christ's joy made you more resilient?

Why does the world have nothing to fear from Christians?

Why does the gospel bring out the worst in the world?

The Evil One

"My prayer is not that you take them out of the
world but that you protect them from the evil
one. They are not of the world, even as I am not
of it." John 17:15-16

J esus prays for the church's protection, for the safety of the first
disciples, and all those who follow in their stead. "Holy Father,
protect them by the power of your name" (John 17:11). "My
prayer" has a way of emphasizing and distilling the mission and
the menace facing the church. The reason for the apparent long de-
lay of Christ's second coming is embedded in this missional prayer
that echoes the Lord's Prayer: "Your kingdom come, your will be
done, on earth as it is in heaven." We are no longer at home in our
home culture. We are chosen outsiders and resident aliens on a
mission that draws opposition from the evil one.

Worldly believers are a bit blasé on the hostility of the world
and the power of the evil one. Over-spiritualizing the reality of
evil may be a problem in some circles, but the greater problem is
underestimating the power of the devil, or even believing that he
exists. Jesus called the evil one "the prince of this world" (John
14:30) and the Apostle John said, "the whole world is under the
control of the evil one" (1 John 5:19). Lurking behind the facade of
civilization is an evil that defies imagining. Human culpability plus
demonic activity magnifies and compounds evil beyond human
calculation. "Enemy-occupied territory—that is what the world
is," wrote C. S. Lewis, and its "rightful king" is "calling us all to

take part in a great campaign of sabotage."[1] The devil's philosophy is easily understood, wrote Lewis in *Screwtape Letters*, "Once you have made the world an end, and faith a means, you have almost won your man, and it makes very little difference what kind of worldly end he is pursuing."[2]

On the subject of the devil the Bible gives us enough information to be on guard, but not enough to indulge our curiosity. Markus Barth observes, "Though [the devil] is often mentioned in the Bible, it is impossible to derive an ontology, phenomenology, and history of Satan sufficiently complete to create a 'satanology' which in the slightest measure corresponds to the weight of biblical 'theo-logy.'"[3] We were meant to be aware of the devil and the power of evil, but never engrossed in the subject. For example, no one need be a student of pornography to be on guard against pornography. To dwell on pornography would be to become its victim. Likewise with the devil, demonic power is real, but should not be fixated on. The spirit of the antichrist pervades the world but as John reminds us, "Greater is he that is in you than he that is in the world" (1 John 4:4).

At the outset of his mission, Jesus made an oblique reference to the devil when he said that the strong man must first be bound before plundering his home (Matt 12:29; Mark 3:27). His comment was more explicit when the seventy-two disciples return rejoicing in their power over the demons. Jesus said, "I saw Satan fall like lightning from heaven" (Luke 10:18). And then shortly before the upper room experience, Jesus gave this summary statement: "Now is the time for judgment on this world; now the prince of this world will be driven out. And I, when I am lifted up from the earth, will draw all people to myself" (John 12:31-32). The binding of Satan means that the church is free to "make disciples of all nations" (Matt 28:18-20). Satan's power is checked by the Spirit of Christ. His demonic influence is curtailed, but remains pervasive.

1. Lewis, *Mere Christianity*, 46.
2. Lewis, *Screwtape Letters*, 35.
3. Barth, *Ephesians*, 228.

Evil's hideous strength is not only fearsome and tyrannical, it is also thrilling and beautiful. There is a seductive side to evil that the inhabitants of the earth find attractive and compelling. The devil's influence is felt not only in violent acts of terrorism but in sky-rocketing sales of pharmaceuticals and warheads. The oppressive world system legitimizes abortions-on-demand and turns children into immortality symbols. Evil is in the dark alley mugging and evil is in the corporate windfall. There is a bull market on Wall Street and poverty runs rampant. The street-wise pimp and the corporate CEO have something in common. The pervasiveness of evil and the universal sweep of idolatry fits the Apostle Peter's description of the devil on the prowl (1 Pet 5:8-9).

Our most graphic images of the devil's persistent power come from the apostle John's Revelation. The image of a raging torrent threatening the bride of Christ captures the nature of the devil's oppression. "Then from his mouth the serpent spewed water like a river, to overtake the woman and sweep her away with the torrent" (Rev 12:15). The world is drowning in the devil's deception. The serpent is spewing out lies and accusations. The sheer volume of deceptive words is overwhelming. The world is inundated by a constant flood of words and ideas inimical to Christ and his kingdom. No place is safe from the barrage of false ideologies and powerful cultural messages that belittle and strive to override the testimony of Jesus.

During the curtailment of the devil's deception the church remains an embattled church of martyrs witnessing to the power of the gospel. The church thrives on the promise of Christ: "I will build my church, and the gates of hell will not overcome it." The church turns "the keys of the kingdom of heaven" and opens the door on a new reality (Matt 16:18-19). In the tension between "the already and the not yet" the church humbly lives in two worlds, the one that is dying and the one that groans for the new birth.

Reflections on the Way

How would a more biblical understanding of evil make disciples more resilient?

What does it mean to you to be in the world but not of the world?

Describe the "beautiful" side of evil. How can we resist the seductive power of evil?

How can the church in the world but not of the world thrive?

DAY 28

Faithful Presence

"They are not of the world, even as I am
not of it." John 17:16

J esus embodies the true nature of the believer's other-worldliness.
His life sets the standard of what it means to be in the world, but
not of the world. We look to Jesus: his compassion and his con-
frontation, his outreach and his withdrawal, his embrace and his
rejection, his teaching and his silence. The way to be in the world
but not of the world is to become like Jesus. We move through the
Gospels prayerfully asking how he did it. We read the book of Acts
to see how the early church did it. We read the epistles to hear from
the apostles on how we should do it. We need plenty of wisdom on
this subject. The fact that Jesus compared his disciples to himself
poses an incredible challenge. How can we begin to be in world,
but not of the world, the way Jesus was. How can we make his
other-worldliness for *the sake of the world* the model for our faithful
presence in the world?

To be in the world but not of the world is not easily done.
We may take pride in our conservative theology and our staunch
moral stand but be downright worldly in our neglect of the poor
and in our greedy ambition for wealth. Our doctrinal stance may
be orthodox, but our devotion to sports and material success may
be idolatrous. We may never miss a Sunday worship service, but
we spend the rest of the week living for self. In the name of pa-
triotism we may wrap the cross in the American flag. "Instead of

being in the world but not of it, we easily become of the world but not in it."[1]

Escape from the world is not an option. So building churches that function as self-contained communities is probably not the best idea. Jesus intended for us to live in the neighborhood, befriending and serving others. The disciple's place is in the world, building, policing, teaching, healing, inventing, and farming. We are ambassadors for Christ, called not to conform to the world, but to be transformed by the renewing of our minds, so that we will be able "to test and approve what God's will is—his good, pleasing and perfect will" (Rom 12:1-2).

Diognetus gives us a moving second century description of the Christian life: "Christians are distinguished from other people neither by country, nor language, nor the customs which they observe . . . following the customs of the natives in respect to clothing, food, and the rest of their ordinary conduct, they display to us their wonderful and confessedly striking (paradoxical) method of life. They dwell in their own countries, but simply as sojourners. As citizens they share in all things with others, and yet endure all things as if foreigners. Every foreign land is to them as their native country, and every land of their birth as a land of strangers. They marry, as do all; they beget children; but they do not destroy their offspring. They have a common table, but not a common bed. They are in the flesh, but they do not live after the flesh. They pass their days on earth, but they are citizens of heaven. They obey the prescribed laws, and at the same time surpass the laws by their lives. They love all people, and are persecuted by all. They are unknown and condemned. . . . They are poor, yet make many rich . . . they are dishonored, and yet in their very dishonor are glorified. They are evil spoken of, and yet are justified; they are reviled and bless; they are insulted, and repay the insult with honor; they do good, yet are punished as evil doers." Diognetus sums it up this way: "*what the soul is in the body . . .Christians are in the world.*"[2]

1. Horton, "How the Kingdom Comes," 46.
2. Quoted in White, *Christian Ethics*, 20

Pastor Jim Belcher encourages "resident aliens" to become bilingual. We need a working knowledge of two languages: the common grace language that engages culture with the conviction that all people are image-bearers of God. This common grace language encourages us to relate to all people as beneficiaries of the Great Commandment and the Great Commission. We also need to know the kingdom of God language that seeks to evangelize men and women with the gospel of Jesus Christ and edify the countercultural community of the Body of Christ.

Sociologist James Hunter reminds believers that the "intermingling of Christian practice and worldly power" produces an inherent complexity. The tensions between assimilation and syncretism are inevitable and even though "unavoidable failure awaits even the most faithful Christians we do not give up."[3] We take to heart the admonition, "Come out of her, my people, so that you will not share in her sins" (Rev 18:4). We heed the counsel "to abstain from sinful desires, which wage war against the soul" (1 Pet 2:11). We make it our aim to "live such good lives among the pagans that, though they accuse [us] of doing wrong, they may see [our] good deeds and glorify God . . ." (1 Pet 2:12). We are ready "to work out [our] salvation with fear and trembling, for it is God who works in [us] to will and to act in order to fulfill his good purpose" (Phil 2:12-13). This is the spiritual direction that applies to the operating room nurse who refuses to participate in late-term abortions, and to the car mechanic whose employer bills for new parts when he uses old replacement parts, and to the hedge-fund investor whose two million dollar end of year bonus challenges his kingdom priorities, and to the mother of three, facing the suburbanite pressure to spend all her time shuttling kids from one activity to another.

To be the faithful presence Christ calls us to be is bound to set us apart as resident aliens, as strangers in our home culture. And even though a Christian may be hard-working, trustworthy, loving, dependable, supportive, and selfless, the world often focuses on the negative differences. "They are surprised that you do not

---

3. Hunter, *To Change the World*, 184.

join them in their reckless, wild living, and they heap abuse on you" (1 Pet 4:4).

The world is the world. Don't worry about the world, the world will worry about itself. Focus on the Jesus way. Instead of trying to change the world, be the people of God in the world. Instead of worrying about what the world thinks, instead of growing angry about what the world does, be concerned about living according to God's will. Instead of focusing on the badness of the world focus on the goodness of God. We have our hands full "purifying" ourselves "by obeying the truth" (1 Pet 1:22). If the church spent more time ridding itself of "all malice and all deceit, hypocrisy, envy, and slander" then she would have a far greater impact in the world. "Only by making our home with Jesus will we be able to distinguish between good and bad worldliness."[4]

Reflections on the Way

Why is being "conservative" not the antidote to worldliness that we often think it is?

How did Jesus engage the world without becoming like the world?

What does Jim Belcher mean when he encourages Christians to become bilingual?

How should Christ's followers determine to impress the world?

4. Bruner, *John*, 993.

DAY 29

Consecration

"Sanctify them by the truth; your word is truth. As you sent me into the world, I have sent them into the world. For them I sanctify myself, that they too may be truly sanctified." John 17:17-19

On a trip to Israel with a group of pastors I read Jesus' prayer of consecration at the Garden Tomb in Jerusalem. We had spent a week in Galilee and a week in Jerusalem. Ten Birmingham pastors and myself were heading home the next morning. It was fitting that we should read Jesus' prayer at the traditional site of his resurrection. We asked the Lord to set aside the bread and cup in our celebration of Holy Communion and then ourselves to his holy purpose. We embraced the truth that our sanctification is rooted in the very one "whom the Father set apart as his very own and sent into the world" (John 10:36). Jesus prays to the Father to do for us what he did for the Son: "Sanctify them by the truth; your word is truth." He is the "Word made flesh," "the Way, the Truth, and the Life," who reveals "the only true God" with the very words the Father gave him (John 1:14; 14:6; 17:3, 8). He is the giver of the Spirit of Truth and we are "saved through the sanctifying work of the Spirit and through belief in the truth" (2 Thess 2:13). Our holiness is exclusively "through the sacrifice of the body of Jesus Christ once for all" (Heb 10:10). There are two consecrations, his and ours, and our "consecration depends absolutely on his."[1] Jesus' atoning sacrifice is the means by which we are "taken up

1. Newbigin, *The Light Has Come*, 232.

into his perfect consecration to the Father and sent into the world to continue, not only by verbal proclamation but also by common life which embodies the same consecration, his total consecration of love and obedience to the Father."[2]

Graduation ceremonies at Beeson Divinity School include a worship service of consecration. Each student is prayed over by the entire faculty. Words of benediction and blessing, thanksgiving and encouragement, are offered in the name of the Father, Son, and Holy Spirit. We pray that the Word of Christ may dwell in them richly and that the peace of Christ may rule in their hearts, and that whatever they do in word or deed they do all in the name of Jesus Christ giving thanks to God the Father through him. After three to four years of serious study of God's Word, these graduates are set aside for mission.

Long before the Word was made flesh and dwelt among us, Jeremiah embodied the Gethsemane mind-set, took up his cross daily, and lived in the power of the resurrection. In his hard-hitting prophetic message, the hope of the gospel prevailed. Jeremiah's life was a parable of Jesus pointing forward to "The Lord Our Righteousness." He embodied the word of the Lord in his life and character. He was not the incarnate one, but he lived an incarnational life.

Jeremiah is our unexpected companion and guide in being the person God calls us to be. We see ourselves "formed," "known," and "set apart," as the prophet was, but we suspect that his appointment "as a prophet to the nations" belongs exclusively to him and not to us. Who are we to think that we have received such a divine appointment? But what was true for Jeremiah is true for us. All believers are God-created, God-known, God-consecrated, and God-commissioned. We have all received the great commission to "go and make disciples of all nations, baptizing them in the name of the Father and of the Son and of the Holy Spirit, and teaching them to obey everything I have commanded you" (Matt 28:19-20).

All of our self-doubts, fears and innumerable inadequacies are answered in the call of God upon our lives. The Lord himself

2. Ibid., 233.

takes the focus of attention off of us—off of our weaknesses and worries, and calls us to himself—to his Word. The Lord drew Jeremiah into his calling the way he draws us into his calling, through a compelling purpose, positive assurance, and the gift of an unambiguous message. Like Jeremiah we are called out of a small world into the large world of God's saving grace. Instead of a life mired in self-pity, self-reliance, feelings of inadequacy and insecurity, the Lord calls us into a great life, a bold life, filled with God's purpose and meaning. Jeremiah shows us what it means to take up our cross and follow the Lord Jesus Christ.

We needed Jesus to pray, "I sanctify myself," because without his sanctification there is no hope for ours. The scholars who insist that we cannot sanctify ourselves are surely right.[3] We cannot say, "I sanctify myself," but we can and must enter into the gift of Christ's sanctification. Augustine saw a parallel "of the same character" between Jesus' "I sanctify myself" and the Apostle Paul's rejoicing "in what I am suffering for you, and I fill up in my flesh what is still lacking in regard to Christ's afflictions, for the sake of his body, which is the church" (Col 1:24).[4]

For twenty years Steve and Sue Befus gave themselves unselfishly to serving the poor in Liberia, West Africa. Steve headed up the medical team at ELWA hospital in Monrovia. Three times the hospital personnel had to be evacuated as rebels closed in, and three times Steve returned to rebuild a hospital looted and ransacked by the enemy he prayed for. On the night of May 1, 1996, Steve thought he would die. He and two other missionaries were stripped and laid on the ground to be shot. But just then another gang of rebels, who were competing for loot, drove up, causing the other group to flee. Steve felt the Lord spared his life that night to provide him with extra time to serve. This gave him the sense of urgency to return to Liberia and rebuild the hospital and renew the ministry.

Many Liberians and westerners recognized Steve's outstanding leadership, but for the most part Steve's ministry went below

3. Bruce, *John*, 731.
4. Augustine, *Homilies on John*, 405.

the radar, as God intended it to be. Steve died in 2003 after an extended struggle with cancer. In his last days he wrote to us, saying, "Many have written that they still pray for a cure, that's fine, I sure wouldn't mind. . . . At this stage in my life it appears that maintaining a life of faith in the months left to me will be a bigger challenge than faith for a cure." At his graveside, I read from Psalm 116, "Precious in the sight of the Lord is the death of his saints." I believe the Lord highly values the life of his saints, but there is also the sense that the Lord finds the death of his saints costly. It is not only we who feel Steve's absence but the Lord himself who pays a costly price in the death of his servant, Steve. This loss is different from the Father giving up the Son, and yet, in the mind of God, it is still related in some special way.

Steve was not given to verbalizing powerful lines, like Jim Elliot's, "He is no fool who gives what he cannot keep to gain what he cannot lose," but he embodied them in his commitment to Christ. In the last few months of his life, 2 Corinthians 4:5-5:9 was his key text: "For what we preach is not ourselves, but Jesus Christ as Lord, and ourselves as your servants for Jesus' sake." His body was weak with cancer, but his spirit was strong. Steve focused on verse ten, "We always carry around in our body the death of Jesus, so that the life of Jesus may also be revealed in our body." Toward the end of his life Steve erased from his computer the record of his emails that chronicled his struggle with cancer. He didn't want that to be the focus. Steve embodied the message; he did not distance himself from the text. "For we who are alive are always being given over to death for Jesus' sake, so that his life may also be revealed in our mortal body. So then death is at work in us, but life is at work in you" (2 Cor 4:11-12).

Reflections on the Way

Do you see yourself sent into the world in the same way the early disciples were?

How is Jeremiah the prophet a model for our discipleship?

Describe how our sanctification is dependent upon Jesus' sanctification.

Whether we are facing terrorists or cancer, how can we demonstrate true dependence on Jesus Christ?

DAY 30

All Believers

"My prayer is not for them alone. I pray also for
those who believe in me through their message,
that all of them may be one, Father, just as you
are in me and I am in you. May they also be in
us so that the world may believe that you have
sent me." John 17:20-21

We have been included in Jesus' prayer of consecration from
the beginning. In Christ, we are in the company of *eternal
lifers* ("that he might give eternal life to all those you have given
him"—John 17:2). "My prayer is not for them alone," offers ret-
roactive approval for blurring the line between the first disciples
and generations of believers who have been given to Christ "out of
the world" and who have obeyed his word. The apostolic disciples
needed to hear this prayer, but so do we. Together we have the
privilege of hearing how Jesus prayed for himself (John 17:1-5), for
his Gospel-writing, epistle-sending apostles (John 17:6-19), and
for all the rest of us (John 17:20-26). We share in the glory and the
security of the Father's love and the Son's joy. We are separated,
sanctified, and sent into the world with the gospel of Jesus Christ.
On the eve of his crucifixion we were on his mind and in his heart.

Before we meditate on the "all" and the "one" we should focus
on the importance of belief. Jesus means for us to believe *personally* in a specific and definable way. He prays for "those who believe
in me through their message." The message does not change. The
salvation we share "was once for all entrusted to God's holy people"

(Jude 3). The "sacred command" was passed on to us (2 Pet 2:21). We have been "born again, not of perishable seed, but of imperishable, through the enduring word of God . . . . And this is the word that was preached to you" (1 Pet 1:23, 25). The Apostle Paul's challenge remains in effect for all believers, "What you heard from me, keep as the pattern of sound teaching, with faith and love in Christ Jesus. Guard the good deposit that was entrusted to you—guard it with the help of the Holy Spirit who lives in us" (2 Tim 1:13-14). This is why Paul said to Timothy, "Guard what has been entrusted to your care," and warned him, "Turn away from godless chatter and the opposing ideas of what is falsely called knowledge, which some have professed and in so doing have departed from the faith" (1 Tim 6:20).

The Word of God—this "imperishable seed" and "good deposit"—is not an end in itself, but the Spirit's provision to guide us into a "devotional, worshipful, eucharistic, vertical" relationship with the Father and the Son.[1] There is nothing doctrinaire and impersonal about this relationship, unless we make it so. We have received the word of God, not as "a human word, but as it actually is, the very Word of God, which is indeed at work in [us] who believe" (1 Thess 2:13). The Word promises to feed our souls: "Very truly I tell you, the one who believes has eternal life. I am the bread of life. . . .Very truly I tell you, unless you eat the flesh of the Son of Man and drink his blood, you have no life in you. Whoever eats my flesh and drinks my blood has eternal life, and I will raise them up at the last day" (John 6:47-54). The Word promises to free our souls: "If you hold to my teaching, you are really my disciples. Then you will know the truth, and the truth will set you free" (John 8:31-32).

This is why the early church "devoted themselves to the apostles' teaching and to the fellowship, to the breaking of the bread and to prayer" (Acts 2:42). Almost every church's denominational distinctives appear represented in the experience of Pentecost and the description of the early church. Roman Catholics see the history of apostolic succession commencing with Peter. Baptists

1. Bruner, *John*, 1007.

point to the baptism of new converts and Pentecostals to the out-pouring of the Holy Spirit. The Reformed tradition resonates with Peter's proclamation of the Word and the believers' devotion to the apostles' teaching. Anglicans and Episcopalians may choose to focus on the breaking of the bread and Methodists on small group fellowships. Mennonites see themselves in the early church's so-cial concern and simple lifestyle. Certain Brethren denominations may emphasize prayer and the Nazarenes may see themselves in the quest for personal holiness. Megachurches identify with the early church's explosive growth. However, the experience of the early church emphasizes not what sets believers apart in denomi-nations, but what holds the followers of Jesus together as the body of Christ. The issue is not our separate denominational distinc-tives, but our shared commitment to the Word of God. The more we focus on Christ and the Gospel the less we will be interested in our denominational distinctives and the more we will cherish the visible unity of the church. "If we walk in the light, as he is the light, we have fellowship one with another" (1 John 1:7).

Jesus prays for the priesthood of *all* believers in the *oneness* of the church. There is only one all-purpose calling for each and every believer and the call to salvation includes the call to sanctification, sacrifice, and simplicity. The call to redemption includes the call to mission and all of our holy vocations. "I urge you to live a life worthy of the calling you have received," urged the Apostle Paul. "Be completely humble and gentle; be patient, bearing with one another in love. Make every effort to keep the unity of the Spirit through the bond of peace. There is one body and one Spirit, just as you were called to one hope when you were called; one Lord, one faith, one baptism; one God and Father of all, who is over all and through all and in all" (Eph 4:1-6).

On the unity of the church, the Apostle Paul was emphatic: "Make every effort to keep the unity of the Spirit through the bond of peace." In English it is hard to do justice to the Greek imperative. It means, "Take pains," "Spare no effort," "Give it all you've got." Obviously Paul intends an all-out effort on our part. A lackadaisi-cal attitude toward the unity of the body of Christ has no place.

Any hint of indifference or passivity is ruled out. Paul calls for "a diligence tempered by all deliberate speed. Yours is the initiative! Do it now! Mean it! You are to do it! I mean it!—such are the overtones in this verse."[2] The big question is how do we keep the unity of the Spirit through the bond of peace, when there is so much that threatens to pull us apart? We know that Paul was vigilant against doctrinal error and disobedience, yet he was also patient and forbearing with the foibles, personalities, and eccentricities of individuals in the body of Christ. This is a challenge for us, because we are tempted to look the other way when presented with cases of heresy and immorality in the church and yet fixate on petty issues and personality clashes in the church. We tend to ignore what we should deal with and deal with what we should ignore.

Reflections on the Way

How should we respond to Jesus' conversation on the way?

Do you see ways in which God is bringing believers together?

Why is the credibility of Jesus' testimony tied to the oneness of the body of Christ?

How can we make every effort to keep the unity of the Spirit in the bond of peace?

2. Barth, *Ephesians*, 428.

DAY 31

The Credible Gospel

"I have given the glory that you gave me, that they may be one as we are one—I in them and you in me—so that they may be brought to complete unity. Then the world will know that you sent me and have loved them even as you have loved me."

John 17:22-23

Jesus is ready now to pray for the world, and he does so by praying for the oneness of all believers. He prays that they will be locked in together like the Father and the Son, so that the world may believe that the Father sent the Son. The way to unity "lies through personal union with the Lord so deep and real as to be comparable with His union with the Father."[1] The good news is that we are able to love one another because we have been loved first. Jesus' prayer for unity parallels his upper room new commandment love. "Love one another. As I have loved you, so you must love one another. By this everyone will know that you are my disciples, if you love one another" (John 13:34-35). Only this time, Jesus ups the ante, instead of everyone knowing we are his disciples, everyone will know that he came from the Father. Jesus puts his own credibility on the line, when he ties the oneness of all believers to the mission of the church. This is a tall order that requires constant vigilance. "It is this visible unity which will bring the world to believe (John 17:21) and know (John 17:23) what

1. Temple, *Readings in St. John's Gospel*, 327.

otherwise it does not and cannot know (John 17:25), namely, God himself in his revelation as the Father of Jesus."[2]

As incredible as it may seem, we are the answer to Jesus' prayer for the world. The mission of the church is to convince the world of the exclusive truth claim of Jesus Christ ("That you sent me"). "When people believe that *God* (and no one else) sent *Jesus* (and no one else) in *the* mission of salvation—then people are finally at home with life's central reality. The church does everything she can—from faithful preaching and praying to loving outreach and service—to seek this faith in a deceived and uncentered world."[3]

Jesus sums up the means to achieving this world-saving mission in a single word, *glory.* "I have given them the glory that you gave me . . ." This is the mutually empowering glory of the Father and the Son (John 17:1), the glory of the real presence of God (17:5), and the glory of the people of God (17:10). This is the glory to be found in the Word, given by the Father (17:6), accepted and obeyed by the church (17:6, 8), opposed by the world (17:14), and received as the truth (17:17). This is the glory to be found in the name, disclosing the full revelation of the words and works of the one true and living God (17:6) and revealing the power of God to save and protect (17:11, 12). This is the glory to be found in the mission of the church, ordained by the Father, commissioned by the Son, and empowered by the Holy Spirit (17:18; 14:16-17; 16:8-14).

The Lord has not left it to us to imagine how we might glorify him. We cannot manufacture our own version of glory and label it "the glory of God." The Israelites did that with their golden calf religion and it didn't work out so well. God's glory is rooted in the Word of God, the name of God, and the mission of God. Many believers seek to do for God what God doesn't want done. Cathedrals are built, ball games played, concerts performed, rigorous ascetic practices are observed, and sermons are preached, all allegedly for the glory of God. But the glory of God is not whatever we think it is, but what God says it is. For the student athlete to glorify God

2. Newbigin, *The Light Has Come,* 235.

3. Bruner, *John,* 1008. (Emphasis his.)

does not mean spending most of his week pumping iron or giving everything he has on game day. God never said he wanted the athlete to leave his heart out on the playing field. He wants his heart for himself. To glorify God does not mean pointing to the sky or taking a knee for Jesus. Nor does it mean giving a shout-out for Jesus after the game. God doesn't need our publicity; God desires our witness. There is a difference between publicity and witness, just as there is a difference between knowing about God and knowing God, and the difference is defined biblically. If we want to know how to glorify God, Jesus' upper room discipleship sermon is a great place to turn.

Forgiveness is key. God's mission to the world is all about forgiveness: to love as we have been loved; to forgive as we have been forgiven. The fifth petition of the Lord's Prayer, "And forgive our debts as we have forgiven our debtors," corresponds to our Lord's prayer, "May they also be in us so that the world may believe that you have sent me" (John 17:21). When Jesus appeared to the disciples after his resurrection, he breathed on them and said, "Receive the Holy Spirit. If you forgive anyone's sins, their sins will be forgiven; if you do not forgive them, they are not forgiven" (John 20:22-23). The oneness of all believers depends upon the work of forgiveness. The Apostle Paul said, "Clothe yourselves with compassion, kindness, humility, gentleness and patience. Bear with each other and forgive one another if any of you has a grievance against someone. Forgive as the Lord forgave you. And over all these virtues put on love, which binds them all together in perfect unity" (Col 3:12-13).

Faithfulness is also key. Of God and his purposes we can be certain; of the changing circumstances of our situation, we can never be but uncertain. Karl Barth reminds us, "I believe—not in myself—I believe in God the Father, the Son and the Holy Ghost." Faith delivers us from trust in ourselves, in our circumstances, and in any other anchor. "We shall never be true to ourselves. . . . In God alone is there faithfulness, and faith is the trust that we may hold to Him, to His promise and to His guidance."[4] Oswald Chambers

---

4. Barth, *Dogmatics in Outline*, 19.

says that "gracious uncertainty" is the mark of the believer's life. "To be certain of God means that we are uncertain in all our ways, not knowing what tomorrow may bring." Chambers adds, "This is generally expressed with a sigh of sadness, but it should be an expression of breathless expectation. . .When we have the right relationship with God, life is full of spontaneous, joyful uncertainty and expectancy."[5]

This is how Jesus loves the world: he prays for all believers to be one in order to convince the world that he has been sent by the Father as the sole means of salvation for the world. The incredible good news of God's sacrificial love is tightly wrapped up in our love for one another. For the sake of the world, Jesus prays, "that they may brought to complete unity" (John 17:23). Surprisingly, this is how God has determined to prove to the world that he loves the world as much as he loves the Son. This shocking truth is consistent with the familiar truth that God so loved the world that he gave his one and only Son (John 3:16), but it is not as readily recognized and embraced by Christ's disciples. Jesus' prayer of consecration is more radical than we imagined.

Reflections on the Way

How does Jesus expect to convince the world that he is the sole means of the salvation of the world?

What is the tangible, visible expression of the glory of God in the church?

Where does the unity of the body of Christ matter most?

How does Jesus' prayer change your perspective on the church?

5. Chambers, *My Utmost For His Highest*, April 29.

DAY 32

Reunion

"Father, I want those you have given me to be with
me where I am, and to see my glory, the glory you
have given me because you loved me before the
creation of the world." John 17:24

A n old and good friend on the West Coast is battling cancer.
He has been through surgery and repeated rounds of chemo-
therapy and experimental trials but the cancer continues to grow.
This morning I have Dan in mind when I hear Jesus pray "I very
much want that special group of people that you gave me to be
with me where I am . . ." A new friend's father died yesterday. I
think of Rick's dad when I hear Jesus pray, ". . . so that they can
see the very special glory that you gave me because you loved me
before the foundation of the world."[1]

Jesus' departure frames the entire upper room experience.
"The hour had come for him to leave this world and go to the Father" (John 13:1). When Jesus said, "Where I am going, you cannot come," a perplexed Peter asked, "Lord, where are you going?"
(John 13:36). His consternation was understandable given his limited vantage point. Jesus sought to comfort his disciples. "Do not
let your hearts be troubled. . . . If I go and prepare a place for you.
I will come back and take you to be with me that you also may be
where I am" (John 14:1,3). A literal, physical, tangible, face-to-face
reunion has always been the promise to Jesus' followers. Augustine
began his exposition on this verse with these words: "The Lord

1. Bruner, *John*, 1010.

Jesus raises up His people to a great hope, a hope that could not possibly be greater. Listen and rejoice in hope, that, since the present is not a life to be loved, but to be tolerated, you may have the power of patient endurance amid all of its tribulation. Listen, I say, and weigh well to what it is that our hopes are exalted. . . . He who overcame the world, says of those for whom He overcame it: listen, believe, hope, desire what He saith: 'Father, I will that they whom you have given me be with me where I am.'"[2]

Dale Bruner links the sixth petition of the Lord's Prayer, "Lead us not into temptation but deliver us from the Evil One," to this special line in Jesus' prayer, "Father, I want the community you gave me to be with me where I am" (John 17:24). "We pray for both temporal and final rescue from the Tempter and so both temporal and final union with Christ in God's glory."[3] This is more than a wish. Jesus is bold in his desire to have all of his disciples join him. He expresses his will "majestically."[4] Jesus is confident that "the will of the Father and the Son is one."[5] Within the next hour or so, Jesus will pray, "not my will, but your will be done," but here he prays, "'I will that where I am they also may be with me.' He came not to do His own will; but He knows that this for which He longs is the Father's will; so at the height of His prayer of self-dedication He can present to the Father His own desire."[6] Praying for himself in Gethsemane, Jesus is conflicted. Praying for his disciples, he is certain. William Temple adds, "Indeed it is only at such a moment, when we have no desire which is not His, that we can safely and confidently present in our prayers our own desires."[7]

Jesus wants all those whom the Father has given him to *behold* his glory. Believing "that you sent me" (John 17:8) means beholding "the glory you have given me because you loved me before the creation of the world" (John 17:24). Believing gives way

2. Augustine, *Homilies on John*, 412.

3. Bruner, *John*, 961.

4. Brown, *John*, 772.

5. Augustine, *Homilies on John*, 413.

6. Temple, *Readings in St. John's Gospel*, 329.

7. Ibid.

to beholding. There are some who would drive a wedge between believing and beholding. As if believing is all explanation and beholding is all expectation. But I would caution against this divorce. If you do not believe you will not behold. Explanation and expectation go hand-in-hand. Faith is the earnest expectation of sight!

Beholding the glory of Christ is a many-faceted experience. So that when we read, "The Word was made flesh and dwelt among us and we beheld his glory, the glory of the only begotten of the Father full of grace and truth" (John 1:14), we can include the full range of Jesus' ministry: his miraculous signs, his teaching and preaching, his lowly service, his cross and resurrection. Jesus on bended knee washing the disciples feet is all part of his glory.

But the glory intended here is "the majesty and splendor that will be His in the life to come,"[8] because it is the "glory that he had with the Father before the world began."[9] This is the glory described in Hebrews: "The Son is the radiance of God's glory and the exact representation of his being, sustaining all things by his powerful word" (Heb 1:3). This is the glory revealed in John's vision of Christ: "When I saw him, I fell at his feet as though dead. Then he placed his right hand on me and said: 'Do not be afraid. I am the First and the Last. I am the Living One; I was dead, and now look, I am alive for ever and ever! And I hold the keys of death and Hades" (Rev 1:17-18). To *behold* is to "contemplate with adoration" the glory of God. We can hardly imagine "the infinite joy of the finite soul," but that is what Jesus prays for.[10]

The apostles thrive on this hope and encourage us to do the same. "If we died with him, we will also live with him" (2 Tim 2:11). The Apostle John wrote, "Dear friends, now we are children of God, and what we will be has not yet been made known. But we know that when Christ appears, we shall be like him, for we shall see him as he is. All who have this hope in him purify themselves, just as he is pure" (1 John 3:2-3). Their focus is on the inheritance to come, the believer's eschatological hope, and the culmination of

8. Bruce, *John,* 736.

9. Carson, *John,* 569.

10. Temple, *Readings in St. John's Gospel,* 330.

our salvation when Christ comes again. "Now if we are children, then we are heirs—heirs of God and co-heirs with Christ, if indeed we share in his sufferings in order that we may also share in his glory" (Rom 8:17). On this side of eternity the apostles envision a sacrificial life of holy obedience rather than material success and the fulfillment of the American dream.

First Peter's opening doxology gives believers three reasons to live for Christ in a difficult culture. We have a *living hope*, a *lasting inheritance*, and a *coming salvation*. There is no room here for a beleaguered and fearful Christian fighting for his life or for a group of Christians lamenting their lost place in the world. We have been given new birth into a living hope and a lasting inheritance that can never perish, spoil or fade. On this side of eternity we catch glimpses of this glory. The Apostle Paul was hopeful, "And we all, who with unveiled faces contemplate the Lord's glory, are being transformed into his image with ever-increasing glory, which comes from the Lord, who is the Spirit" (2 Cor 3:18). I wish I had Jesus' reunion prayer in mind when I talked with my dear friend Dan last night.

> "Even as I already now experience in my heart the beginning of eternal joy, so after this life I still have perfect blessedness such as no eye has seen, no ear has heard, no human heart has ever imagined: a blessedness in which to praise God forever" (Heidelberg Catechism Q and A 58).

Reflections on the Way

How does the promise of the real reunion with Christ and all the other reunions encompassed in his promise impact your life?

Why is the beauty and wonder of beholding tied to believing?

What is the evidence of being truly inspired and energized by this hope?

How does Jesus' glory prayer encourage the living and the dying?

DAY 33

Knowing God

> "Righteous Father, though the world does not know you, I know you, and they know that you have sent me. I have made you known to them and will continue to make you known in order that the love you have for me may be in them and that I myself may be in them." John 17:25-26

Each time we hear Jesus pray to the "Father" we hear the focus of his prayer and we feel the intimacy of the divine conversation. When Jesus prays to the "Holy Father" (John 17:11) and the "Righteous Father," he reveals the divine attributes of holy discernment and just discrimination. Jesus shares the Father's righteous discrimination. The world is on one side and Jesus and his followers are on the other.

Churches that choose not to distinguish between Christ and the world obscure the meaning of conversion. They find the distinction between believers and unbelievers unwelcome. But Jesus sets a bold boundary between himself and the world for the sake of the world and expects us to do the same. Nothing is gained by pretending that the world knows the Father when it doesn't. To pray, "the world does not know you," confirms the truth proclaimed in the prologue, "He was in the world, and though the world was made through him, the world did not recognize him. He came to that which was his own, but his own did not receive him" (John 1:10-11). This assessment corresponds to Jesus' earlier statement that world's peace is not his peace (John 14:27) and explains why the world hates Jesus and his disciples (John 15:18). "They will treat you this way because of my name, for they do not know the one who sent me" (John 15:21).

However, the bad news, "though the world does not know you," is far outweighed by the good news, "I know you, and they know that you have sent me." The prepositional phrase, "though the world does not know you," is not intended to belittle the world's rejection or bemoan the failure of Jesus' ministry. It is simply a fact acknowledged by Jesus in his prayer of consecration that encourages all believers everywhere to see themselves as "chosen outsiders" and "resident aliens" in an unbelieving world. The followers of Jesus Christ have always been marginalized and this will remain true until Christ comes again. What is significant is how Jesus frames the world's unbelief. It is gathered up into an impersonal collective—the world. The world remains the world. We are not going to change the world. But there is hope that people in the world, people for whom Christ died, "will cease to be the world and will join those of whom Jesus says for they are yours."[1] This is why the apostle Paul wrote, "So from now on we regard no one from a worldly point of view" (2 Cor 5:16).

Knowing God is very different from knowing about God.[2] We can know a whole lot about theology, godliness, the Bible, and church history, without ever knowing God. Information about God is decidedly different from truly knowing God. Unless Jesus' prayer is true, "I have made you known to them," we really do not know God at all. No disciple can ever take credit for thinking their way into the kingdom of God. God takes the initiative to makes himself known personally. We are all dependent upon the Spirit of truth to guide us into all truth. Every conversion is a miracle of God's grace. Every conversion is a virgin birth.

The *knowing* that Jesus promises is continuous and life-changing. Jesus is about to reveal the full extent of God's love in the Cross, and the power of God's love in the resurrection, and the truth of God's love in the outpouring of the Holy Spirit. This

1. Carson, *John*, 561.
2. Packer, *Knowing God*, 21.

is the deep knowing of his abiding presence and his transforming love. Jesus prays that the love the Father has for him will be given to us so that the love we have for one another will be the love of the triune God. Loving parents want to see their love translated into the lives of their children. Our heavenly Father wants this, too. We are not simply the objects of God's love, but the recipients of his transforming love that turns God's love for his Son into our love for one another.[3] God loves us with a love that makes us loving. What makes this love so great is that we are not the source of this love. God is the source. This is the love that abounds "more and more in knowledge and depth of insight, so that we may be able to discern what is best and may be pure and blameless for the day of Christ, filled with the fruit of righteousness that comes through Jesus Christ—to the glory and praise of God" (Phil 1:9-11). This is the love that the world can neither discern nor destroy, for nothing in this world "will be able to separate us from the love of God that is in Christ Jesus our Lord" (Rom 8:39). Jesus ends his prayer on the same note that he began the upper room experience, "Having loved his own who were in the world, he loved them to the end" (John 13:1).

Reflections on the Way

Why does unbelief deserve to be defined for the sake of the world?

What is the difference between the knowledge about God and the knowledge of God?

How can the love of God be the love with which we love one another?

If we love others the way Christ loves us, will people put their faith in us or God?

3. Carson, *John*, 570.

DAY 34

The Valley

"When he had finished praying, Jesus left with
his disciples and crossed the Kidron Valley. On
the other side there was a garden, and he and his
disciples went into it." John 18:1

When Jesus finished praying *out loud*, he and his disciples
crossed the Kidron Valley. It is hard to imagine that Jesus
stopped praying as they descended into the valley from the Temple
Mount and climbed the western slope of the Mount of Olives. He
had traversed this valley with these disciples many times before.
As they walked down into the valley did the twenty-third Psalm
come to Jesus' mind? "Even though I walk through the deepest,
darkest valley, I will fear no evil, for you are with me; your rod
and staff they comfort me." On any given Sunday someone in the
household of faith is descending into the valley and climbing up
the other side to Gethsemane.

The agony of Gethsemane was unique to Jesus and we do not
wish to minimize that uniqueness, but it is also true that all believers descend into the valley and end up on their knees in Gethsemane praying, "Not my will, but your will be done." I remember
being there when my father was dying. I knew that "the Spirit helps
us in our weakness" and I knew that even though I didn't know
how I ought to pray, "the Spirit himself intercedes for us through
wordless groans. . . . in accordance with the will of God" (Rom
8:26-27).

Jesus may have recalled King David's escape from Absalom, when he was forced by his son's treachery to flee Jerusalem and cross the Kidron Valley (2 Sam 15:23). The high priest and Levites were prepared to travel into the wilderness with the ark of the covenant, but David protested, "Take the ark of God back into the city. If I find favor in the Lord's eyes, he will bring me back and let me see it and his dwelling place again. But if he says, 'I am not pleased with you,' then I am ready; let him do to me whatever seems good to him'" (2 Sam 15:25-26). David's words and the silent prayer behind them seem to point forward to Jesus' Gethsemane prayer. Tradition links Psalm 3, David's prayer for deliverance, with this heart-wrenching episode. David begins, "Lord, how many are my foes! How many rise up against me! Many are saying of me, 'God will not deliver him'" (Ps 3:1). But David is confident that he will be delivered: "Arise, Lord! Deliver me, my God! Strike all my enemies on the jaw; break the teeth of the wicked" (Ps 3:7). If Jesus has this prayer in mind he knows that deliverance will come only after he has died for the very enemies who are striking him on the jaw and nailing him to a cross.

We have spent so much time with Jesus in the upper room that it is easy for us to forget that just two days before Jesus had crossed the Kidron Valley to preach his Sermon on the End of the World (Matt 24:1-25:46). The occasion for the sermon was his leaving the temple for the last time and the setting of the sermon was the Mount of Olives. Jesus was hot—agitated, accusatory, fierce in tone and temper. He burned with anger against the teachers of the law and the Pharisees for their hypocrisy, showy piety, and hostility to the revelation of God. He called them names: "You hypocrites! You snakes! You brood of vipers!" He blamed them for the blood of the prophets from the blood of righteous Abel to the blood of Zechariah. His parting words were, "For I tell you, you will not see me again until you say, 'Blessed is he who comes in the name of the Lord'" (Matt 23:39). All of this is in Jesus' mind as he descends into the valley.

Zambian New Testament scholar Joe Kapolyo emphasizes the significance of Jesus turning his back on Judaism and abandoning the whole sacrificial system.[1] What Jesus refuses to do is turn his back on the Jewish people! The destruction of the temple prophesied in Jesus' Last Sermon signifies not only the end of Judaism but the end of all religions, including Christendom. Only Christ fulfills the human need for salvation and the longing of the soul. If the temple is done away with, how much more will all religious traditions be eclipsed by the presence of Jesus? Jesus is Lord. He is the one who is greater than Judaism, Islam, Hinduism, Confucianism, ancestral worship, and all forms of tribal animism and modern existentialism. The end of the beginning of the last days started when Jesus walked out of the temple and then in three days the curtain of the temple was torn in two (Matt 27:51). "The temple worship of the ancient people of God is all over and the way to God's holy presence has been opened up for all by means of this one sacrifice for the sin of the whole world."[2]

The Sermon on the End of the World is a message for disciples. Jesus calls for discernment, resilience, readiness, obedience, and ministry in the name of Jesus. Don't be deceived, distracted, or confused. Don't become fearful, complacent, lazy, or indifferent to the needs around you. Jesus' message has two themes woven together: no-fear-apocalyptic and fear-of-the-Lord parabolic. Wake up. Keep watch. Stay alert. Be prepared. Invest in God's kingdom work. Make the most of your ministry opportunities! The Sermon on the End of the World and Jesus' discipleship sermons in the upper room and on the streets of Jerusalem have prepared his disciples for the cataclysmic event of the cross and for the seismic impact of the mission of God.

It is hard for us to grasp the tremendous outpouring of Jesus' passion in the days and hours leading up to his descent into the Kidron Valley. He has done everything he could to prepare his disciples. Jesus could not have said what he said without deep emotion: "I am telling you now before it happens, so that when it does happen you will believe that I am who I am" (John 13:19); "I have told you this so that my joy may be in you and that your joy

1. Kapolyo, "Matthew," 1161.

2. Bruner, *Matthew*, vol. 2, 757.

may be complete" (John 15:11); "All this I have told you so that you will not fall away" (John 16:1); "I have much more to say to you, more than you can bear. But when he, the Spirit of truth, comes he will guide you into all truth" (John 16:12); "I have told you these things, so that in me you may have peace" (John 16:33).

The physical descent through the Kidron Valley provided the opportunity Jesus *needed* to transition from preparing the disciples to preparing himself for the cross. He's ready. He's been ready, but he is also physically, emotionally, and spiritually spent. He served the disciples flat-out and now he needs to crash *with the Father*. The exalted tone of his glory prayer, the glory he shared with the Father before the creation of the world, yields understandably to a troubled and sorrowful soul facing not only physical torture but utter spiritual abandonment.

Reflections on the Way

Why did Jesus shift physical locations?

Given all that Jesus has said and prayed what do you think the disciples were experiencing as they crossed the Kidron Valley to Gethsemane?

How did Jesus pour himself into his disciples?

How would you describe the tone of Jesus' glory prayer?

DAY 35

Gethsemane

"Then Jesus went with his disciples to place called
Gethsemane, and he said to them, 'Sit here while
I go over there and pray.' He took Peter and the
two sons of Zebedee along with him, and he began to be sorrowful and troubled. Then he said
to them, 'My soul is overwhelmed with sorrow to
the point of death. Stay here and keep watch with
me.'" Matthew 26:36-38

Gethsemane means "oil press" and is located on the Mount of
Olives in a grove of olive trees. It is here where Jesus appears
pressed beyond all measure. When he stands before Caiaphas,
Pilate, and Herod, we picture Jesus silently resilient in complete command of his emotions, but here in the quiet garden of
Gethsemane his soul is crushed. His demeanor and tone are radically different from what they have been throughout the evening.
The precise site of Gethsemane is a matter of debate among western, Russian, Armenian, and Greek Orthodox church leaders, but
busloads of tourists/pilgrims visit the traditional site daily. The
day I was there the sun was bearing down and it was hot. I sat in
the shade of an olive tree as pilgrims from every nation, tribe, and
people group took their group pictures. Amidst the crowds and
the hushed cacophony of the nations I tried to imagine that singular night when Jesus sought the quiet privacy of the garden to pray.

Jesus remains especially patient with the disciples. Like a par-
ent with children, he continues to guide them. He demands little

and expects less, "Sit here while I go over there to pray." The disciples seem woefully naive of what is about to take place. It's almost as if they're too tired to care. It has been a very long, emotionally draining day filled with tension, self-questioning, and confusion. They have had a week of days like that. A short time ago Jesus acknowledged that they had reached their limit: "I have much more to say to you, more than you can bear" (John 16:12).

Jesus continues to be transparent with the disciples, especially with Peter, James, and John. They were with him when he healed Jairus' daughter and present on the Mount of Transfiguration. This was an inner circle for prayer, not privilege. When the *inner ring*, as C. S. Lewis called it, *exists for exclusion*, we have a problem. But in this case, being part of the inner circle called for greater stamina and spiritual discipline. More humility and self-denial were called for. The inner circle *in Christ* is always more about responsibility than ambition and more about sacrifice than status. Even though they will scatter along with the rest of the disciples, and Peter will deny him three times, Jesus desires their companionship. Even now at the end, Jesus desires to do most everything in community.

Jesus led the three to a secluded part of the garden. He shared with them what they had undoubtedly already observed, "My soul is overwhelmed with sorrow to the point of death. Stay here and keep watch with me." Earlier in the week, Jesus revealed the thin line between conversation with the disciples and communion with the Father, when he said, "Now my soul is troubled and what shall I say? 'Father, save me from this hour'? No, it was for this very reason I came to this hour. 'Father, glorify your name!'" (John 12:27-28).

Martin Luther's description invites us into Christ's Gethsemane grief: "Christ speaks here as mere man struggling in death's throes, seeking for support from his disciples whom he before had often consoled. With tremors and shuddering his heart is overwhelmed with grief, and in despair of life, sensing death, he knows that he must now die and pours out his grief before his disciples.

His deep anguish and need overwhelm him utterly and cause him to take refuge in his disciples who are much weaker than he."[1]

Gethsemane was an essential interlude between the upper room and the cross giving Jesus time to regroup and focus. Jesus was deeply troubled and he was honest *and human* enough to admit it. One of the big reasons we can hold firmly to the faith we profess, is because "we do not have a high priest who is unable to sympathize with our weaknesses, but we have one who has been tempted in every way, just as we are—yet without sin" (Heb 4:15). Dale Bruner calls this "the Magna Carta of depression," reminding us that it is not a sin to be depressed.[2] Sure, sin can cause depression, but not all depression is attributed to sin. Jesus' soul was overwhelmed not because he was feeling sorry for himself. Nor was he troubled by unconfessed sins or by weak faith or by repressed anger. His depression was not due to some undefined sadness or emotional letdown or chemical imbalance. Jesus fought depression in two simple ways: by relating to his close friends, even though their companionship offered little, and by persisting in prayer, even though the Father's will was very difficult. If it was possible for the disciples to know how he prayed, I believe it is possible for us to know why he prayed. Through prayer Jesus grappled with the meaning of his death —"the horrifying cup of vicarious suffering."[3]

Jesus was depressed because he was about to die by crucifixion. The imminent prospect of severe physical abuse and the extreme torture of crucifixion were bound to cause intense emotional pain. Facing death with stoic resolve is one thing, but facing a protracted dying process designed to maximize pain is quite another. Jesus' humanity was real in every sense of the word, which meant that being without sin was not a matter of fate but of faithfulness. Knowing what he was about to endure must have weighed heavily upon him, not only because of the physical pain involved but because of the challenge to his obedience.

1. Luther, *Complete Sermons*, vol. 5, 383.

2. Bruner, *Matthew*, vol. 2, 649.

3. France, *Matthew*, 373.

Jesus was troubled because he was about to die alone, abandoned by his friends and his Father. On the way to Gethsemane, Jesus announced to the disciples that they would all fall away. In Gethsemane he must have contemplated the Father's abandonment. Added to the prospect of extreme physical pain and maximum spiritual endurance was the utter aloneness of this experience.

Jesus was overwhelmed because he was about to die for the sins of the world. Jesus expected "to give his life a ransom for many" (Matt 20:28), and on at least three occasions he explained to his disciples how "he must go to Jerusalem and suffer . . . and be killed" (Matt 16:21). Only now, the full impact of taking upon himself the sin of humanity bore down on him. Can anyone contemplate a descent into hell and not be depressed? His reference to the cup, although stated in a word, alluded to the horrific outpouring of God's wrath upon him.

Jesus' depression was real, his humanity true, his obedience free, and his courage undaunted. Have you ever felt so bad you could die? That is how Jesus felt in Gethsemane. "My soul is overwhelmed with sorrow to the point of death." Because there are so many points of similarity between our grief and Jesus' grief we don't want to distance ourselves from the Gethsemane experience. We can learn about Gethsemane through personal experience, even as we acknowledge that *his* Gethsemane was totally unique.[4] The human experience of God and God's experience of humanity are not mutually exclusive. The author of Hebrews used Jesus' Gethsemane experience to define the strength made perfect in weakness: "During the days of Jesus' life on earth, he offered up prayers and petitions with loud cries and tears to the one who could save him from death, and he was heard because of his reverent submission. Although he was a son, he learned obedience from what he suffered and, once made perfect, he became the source of eternal salvation for all who obey him" (Heb 5:7-9). By virtue of our humanity we all have our Gethsemanes, but by virtue of

4. Chambers, *My Utmost for His Highest*, April 5.

his Gethsemane, we have the expectation of salvation through his death and resurrection.

Reflections on the Way

What does Jesus teach us in Gethsemane about facing our suffering?

How is Jesus' deep anguish a comfort to his disciples?

Are we any better than the three disciples when our brothers and sisters in Christ endure their Gethsemanes?

How does Jesus' Gethsemane experience impact your devotion to Christ?

DAY 36

Watch and Pray

"Going a little farther, he fell with his face to the ground and prayed, 'My Father, if it is possible, may this cup be taken from me. Yet not as I will, but as you will.' Then he returned to his disciples and found them sleeping. 'Couldn't you men keep watch with me for one hour?' he asked Peter. 'Watch and pray so that you will not fall into temptation. The spirit is willing, but the flesh is weak.' He went away a second time and prayed, 'My Father, if it is not possible for this cup to be taken away unless I drink it, may your will be done.' When he came back, he again found them sleeping, because their eyes were heavy. So he left them and went away once more and prayed the third time, saying the same thing. Then he returned to the disciples and said to them, 'Are you still sleeping and resting? Look, the hour has come, the Son of Man is delivered into the hands of sinners. 'Rise! Let us go! Here comes my betrayer!'" Matthew 26:39-46

The disciples had the opportunity to encourage Jesus as well as to learn from him, but they failed to take advantage of either opportunity. The only support they gave him was their sleepy presence. They learned nothing to help them face the trials that they were about to experience. When Jesus returned to the disciples, he asked Peter, "Could you men not keep watch with me for one hour?" Since no response is recorded we imagine Jesus receiving a blank stare from the otherwise outspoken disciple. Undeterred from his constant commitment to their spiritual formation, Jesus said, "Watch and pray so that you will not fall into temptation. The spirit is willing, but the body is weak." If the disciples were soldiers ordered by their commanding officer to stand guard, would they have fallen asleep? I doubt it.

The reaction of the disciples is typical of how we respond to Christ. If our boss asks us to do something, we do it right away because it is our job. If our coach asks you to do something, we do it because we are on the team. If our friend asks us to do something, we drop everything and do it out of friendship. But if our Lord asks us to do something, we sleep on it. In the military, a soldier sleeping at his post would be charged with dereliction of duty, but in the church, a believer feels under no obligation to pray. "Peter's three denials in the courtyard follow Peter's three naps in the garden. If we do not say our prayers, we cannot resist temptations—it is that basic. Gethsemane is almost the ABC of Christian faith; it is Jesus' final summary of his teaching; it is the quintessential Sermon on the Mount. Praying is the center—the open secret—of Christian discipleship."[1]

Through prayer Jesus determined how he would face the suffering that was about to bear down on him. He moves from feeling overwhelmed with sorrow to a firm resolve to obey the Father's will. "In suffering, much depends on how a person decides *to face* the suffering. Once a position is discovered as the will of God, one can sometimes handle what comes with poise."[2] This is the poise that is won through prayer. Jesus' resilience and resolve comes from falling flat on his face before the Father and praying, "My Father, if it is possible, may this cup be taken from me. Yet not as I will, but as you will."

1. Bruner, *Matthew*, vol.2, 657.
2. Ibid., 648.

Like Jesus we pray for the courage to say, and mean it, "Not my will, but your will be done." The simplicity of Jesus' prayer is important. Sincerity is found in the utter simplicity of a heart truly transparent before God. Through our own Gethsemane experiences we come to want what the Lord wants and to desire his will, not our own. There is deep resolve and purpose in the voice of Jesus when he says, "Look, the hour is near, and the Son of Man is betrayed into the hands of sinners." Something awful was about to happen. The Son of Man was about to be handed over to sinners. We have known from the beginning that Jesus came to call sinners to repentance (Mark 2:17; Matt 9:13), and the way he would do that was by giving himself up for them—for us.

We are like the disciples in Gethsemane, but by God's grace, Jesus says, "Get up, let's go!" We deserve to be left behind, but Jesus still wants us. We hardly know the difference between Jesus' strength made perfect in weakness and the disciples' weakness pretending to be strong, but Jesus still calls us to follow him. The one redeeming fact in all of this is that it is Jesus who says, "Get up, let's go!"

Reflections on the Way

Why did Jesus treat the disciples better than they deserved?

Where did Jesus find the courage to go forward?

How can we deepen our resolve to obey the Father's will?

What does it mean to you today to hear Jesus say, "Get up, let's go!"?

DAY 37

Seventy-Thousand Angels

"Then the men stepped forward, seized Jesus and
arrested him. With that, one of Jesus' companions
reached for his sword, drew it out and struck the
servant of the high priest, cutting off his ear. 'Put
your sword back in its place,' Jesus said to him, 'for
all who draw the sword will die by the sword. Do
you think I cannot call on my Father, and he will at
once put at my disposal more than twelve legions
of angels? But how then would the Scriptures be
fulfilled that say it must happen in this way?'"
Matthew 26:50b-54

The prayer Jesus could have prayed is impressive, but what he
prayed is redemptive. Jesus in Gethsemane teaches his disciples two important lessons: one is on *prayer* and the other is on
power. The essence of prayer is "Not my will but your will be done"
and the essence of power is "Not in my way, but in your way"
your will be done. The prayer and power lessons of Gethsemane
underscore the *discipline of surrender* and the *power of God onto
salvation*. Gethsemane teaches us to learn obedience by the things
that we suffer (Heb 5:8) and to "fix our eyes on Jesus, the author
and perfecter of our faith, who for the joy set before him endured
the cross, scorning its shame, and sat down at the right hand of the
throne of God." At his arrest and trial we are drawn to "consider

him who endured such opposition from sinful men, so that [we] will not grow weary and lose heart" (Heb 12:2-3).

All eyes are on Jesus. And even though he is being arrested, he is at the center of the action and in control of the events. Jesus is not a helpless victim in need of Peter's protection. "What happens *happens* only because Jesus deliberately refuses to prevent it, as he could easily do."[1] Jesus literally surrenders to a large crowd armed with swords and clubs, but this is not unusual for him to do. It was what he had been doing from the beginning. The incarnation is a great act of willed passivity, second only to the cross itself. The arrest in the garden is consistent with the meaning and purpose of the incarnation.

Peter played the hero. He drew his sword and struck one of the servants of the high priest, cutting off his ear (John 18:10). Immediately before the incident, Peter was unable to stay awake and pray. Shortly after the arrest, Peter was afraid to admit to a servant girl that he knew Jesus. If Peter had followed his Lord's lead and practiced the discipline of surrender, he would have patiently prayed and clearly confessed. Instead he willfully and foolishly took up the sword. Peter's courage depended upon an ego challenge rather than a spiritual challenge.

Earlier that very night Peter claimed that he was willing to lay down his life for Jesus (John 13:37). The evidence for such a claim was now apparent. Peter drew his sword and cut off the ear of the high priest's servant. Immediately, Jesus commanded Peter, "Put your sword away! Shall I not drink the cup the Father has given me?" (John 18:11). Why was Peter willing to risk his life in hand-to-hand combat in the garden, but afraid to admit to a servant girl that he knew Jesus? This doesn't appear to make sense until one realizes the nature of the conflicting challenges.

In the garden it was a challenge to Peter's bravery, his willingness to fight and his readiness to put his life on the line for the cause. Peter was up to the ego challenge. But alone in the high priest's courtyard, with no surrounding audience, Peter was unwilling to admit that he was one of Jesus' disciples. He was all set to

1. France, *Matthew*, 374.

man-up for the ego challenge, but he shriveled up when it came to the witness challenge. When his own ego was not in question and his macho image was not threatened, Peter found it easy to deny that he ever knew Jesus.[2]

Augustine drew a parallel between Peter's violent action and Moses when he killed the Egyptian who was beating up a Hebrew slave. "Both sinned through love," Augustine said, "the one for his brother, the other for his Lord, through a *carnal* love."[3] Such heroic, self-centered love has no place in Christian discipleship, because it embraces the *cause* more than Christ. Peter aimed for the head and severed the servant's ear. Is there any symbolism here? When the church meets injustice with injustice, fights fire with fire, and returns evil for evil, the net effect is to make it that much harder for people to hear the gospel. One of Jesus' favorite lines was "he who has ears to hear let him hear" and the Apostle Paul asked, "how can they hear without someone preaching to them?" (Rom 10:14). If we are intent on communicating the gospel of Christ, it doesn't make any sense to be cutting off ears! I don't mean that statement literally, but metaphorically. When we engage in violent and defensive behavior that prevents people from hearing the gospel we are figuratively cutting off their ears.

A violent defense of Jesus has no justification under any circumstances. Matthew doesn't even bother to tell us that Jesus healed the servant whose ear was cut off. But John tells us his name and says it was his right ear (John 18:10). Matthew focuses on Jesus' rebuke of Peter, "Put your sword back in its place, for all who draw the sword will die by the sword." There is a place for the sword (Rom 13:4; 1 Pet 2:13-17), but "not in the defense of God or his Christ. Every attempt to defend Jesus' mission by force is doomed to failure."[4]

What looked like utter helplessness to the disciples was in fact absolute strength. Like a soldier having snuck in behind enemy lines, Jesus was in full command of the strategy that would

2. Webster, *The God Who Kneels*, 130

3. Bruner, *John*, 671.

4. Bruner, *John*, 672-673.

ultimately win the war. Jesus in Gethsemane not only teaches us how to pray but how to use power. The meaning and the method are consistent. Jesus doesn't need his disciples fighting for him with the weapons of the world. Jesus seems surprised that Peter doesn't know that he has thousands of battle-ready angels at his immediate disposal. All he has to do is say the word and his Father will make it happen. The problem however with calling in the angel warriors is simple: "How then would the Scriptures be fulfilled that say it must happen in this way?" That is to say, "Peter, don't you know that everything is being orchestrated by divine necessity."

"It must happen just like this." Martin Luther wrote, "Here then is the ground of Christ's suffering: not because he had to, or because God could not find another way to effect his praise and glory, but in order that God might be vindicated as true to his Word which he had spoken through his prophets."[5]

Reflections on the Way

How do you understand the relationship between prayer and power?

Describe the difference between the heroic challenge and the witness challenge?

When the Christian life is motivated more by carnal love rather than redemptive love, what happens?

How does Gethsemane reveal the power of God?

5. Luther, *Complete Sermons of Martin Luther*, vol. 5, 380.

DAY 38

"Forgive Them"

"Jesus said, 'Father, forgive them, for they do not
know what they are doing.'" Luke 23:34

The next time we hear Jesus pray he is on the cross. Of the
seven statements Jesus gave from the cross, three are prayers.
In the hours leading up to the cross, Jesus was mostly silent. He
appeared first before the Sanhedrin, then Pilate, Herod, followed
by Pilate again, all the while saying very little. The prophet Isaiah
spoke of the silence of the Suffering Servant. "He was oppressed
and afflicted, yet he did not open his mouth; he was led like a lamb
to the slaughter, and as sheep before her shearers is silent, so he
did not open his mouth" (Isa 53:7). The silence of Jesus at his trial
and crucifixion is extraordinary. He offered no criticism, gave no
explanation, provided no defense, and uttered no blame. He was
"despised and rejected," but he did not dispute his accusers. He
"took up our infirmities and carried our sorrows" without a word
of indignation or self-pity. He was stricken by God, smitten by
him, and afflicted," yet he opened not his mouth.

On the cross Jesus uttered seven brief sentences. Three are
prayers:

"Father, forgive them." Luke 23:34

"My God, my God! Why have you forsaken me?"
Mark 15:34

"Father, into your hands I commit my spirit."
Luke 23:46

He begins and ends his statements from the cross by calling out to the Father. And in the middle he cries to his God. The second and sixth statements from the cross contemplate the present and the future in the light of eternity. At the point of his greatest physical pain, Jesus contemplates heaven and the accomplishment of the Father's purposes.

> "Today you will be with me in paradise." Luke 23:43

> "It is finished." John 19:30

The third and fifth words from the cross are immediate and practical and reflect the real world concerns of the Savior.

> "Woman, behold your son." John 19:26-27

> "I thirst." John 19:30

We are not surprised by Jesus' readiness to pray and forgive. This is the fundamental purpose of his ministry. This is why he came: "Give him the name Jesus, because he will save his people from their sins" (Matt 1:21). "I have not come to call the righteous, but sinners to repentance" (Luke 5:32). This is what he taught his disciples: "For if you forgive people when they sin against you, your heavenly Father will also forgive you. But if you do not forgive people their sins, your Father will not forgive your sins" (Matt 6:14-15). This is what he preached: "And when you stand praying, if you hold anything against anyone, forgive him, so that your Father in heaven may forgive you your sins" (Mark 11:25). This is what he practiced, "Love your enemies and pray for those who persecute you" (Matt 5:44).

Our communion with God is directly tied to our willingness to embrace God's work of forgiveness. Jesus said, "Love your enemies and pray for those who persecute you" (Matt 5:44); "Bless those who curse you, pray for those who mistreat you" (Luke 6:28). To forgive those who have wronged us is a sign that we have been forgiven. In the light of the cross there is little doubt as to our responsibility to forgive. The Apostle Paul said, "Bear with each other and forgive whatever grievances you may have against one another. Forgive as the Lord forgave you. And over all these virtues put on love, which binds them all together in perfect unity" (Col 3:13-14).

Who did Jesus pray for as he hung on the cross? Did he pray for the soldiers who mocked him and thrust a crown of thorns upon his head? Yes, Jesus prayed for them. Did he pray for Pilate, the Roman governor, who washed his hands in front of the crowd and declared, "I am innocent of this man's blood, it is your responsibility!"? Yes, Jesus earnestly sought the Father on behalf of Pilate. Did he pray for the Galilean pilgrims and the crowds who shouted, "Crucify him! Crucify him!" Did he pray for the Jewish ruling body, the Sanhedrin, who sought to condemn him on false chargers? Did he pray for the chief high priest, who charged him with blasphemy? Yes, Jesus prayed for them all. He prayed for his disciples who scattered and the soldiers who drove spikes through his hands and feet. Yes, Jesus interceded on behalf of everyone.

Did the soldiers know they were crucifying the King of kings and Lord of lords? Did Pilate know that he would one day stand before this very same Jesus, who is seated "at the right hand of the Majesty in heaven" (Heb 1:3)? Did the crowds know that they were jeering at the Lord of Glory? Did the Jews know they were mocking and spitting in the face of their Messiah? Did the disciples know that they were abandoning their soon to be risen Lord? Ignorance may be inexcusable but it remains, thank God, forgivable. Many of those who shouted "Crucify him! Crucify him!" were in the crowd on Pentecost when Peter preached. He declared: "Now, brothers, I know that you acted in ignorance, as did your leaders. But this is how God fulfilled what he had foretold through all the prophets, saying that his Christ would suffer. Repent, then, and turn to God, so that your sins may be wiped out, that times of refreshing may come from the Lord . . ." (Acts 3:17-19).

As surely as Jesus prayed for the Roman soldier pounding the spikes into his hands and feet he prays for you and me. We must see ourselves, along with Pilate, the religious leaders, the angry crowd and the Roman soldiers, in need of forgiveness. When Jesus said, "Father, forgive them for they know not what they do," he prayed for us. It is our sins that nailed Jesus to the cross. "God demonstrates his own love for us in this: While we were still sinners, Christ died for us. . .While we were God's enemies, we were reconciled to him through the death of his Son" (Rom 5:8, 10). Martin Luther used a graphic figure to depict our responsibility in the death of Christ. He said we carry around the nails of Christ's cross in our pocket. We cringe at the very thought of the crucifixion; we hardly feel responsible for spikes driven through the hands and feet of Jesus. But that is what our sins did. He "was pierced for our transgressions, he was crushed for our iniquities; the punishment that brought us peace was upon him, and by his wounds we are healed . . . the Lord has laid on him the iniquity of us all" (Isa 53:5-6).

I have never met anyone who mourned more painfully and in greater agony than David Conner. The lines on his face seemed frozen and contorted in a cry of pain. His eyes, swollen and red, filled with a seemingly endless supply of tears. When he spoke, the trembling of his lips seemed to spread throughout his body. He shivered as if he was always cold. I believe David grieved over his sin as deeply as anyone could grieve. And when I visited him in prison, even his faint smile seemed to hurt. David was in prison because he accidentally killed a mother and child on a two-lane road in Indiana. It was a Saturday afternoon and David had been drinking. He was impatient and ticked off at a motorcyclist who had passed him on a curve. He sped up to pass and lost control on the next curve. He hit the oncoming car head-on. The mother and child died instantly. It was as if in the twinkling of an eye David entered hell itself. Every evil thing he had ever done was now dumped into his despairing soul. How could a human being do what he had done? He went from being an ordinary husband and average father to being the very personification of evil. Overnight he became an object of hate in our small town. The victim's family could not have condemned David more if he had been solely responsible for the Nazi Holocaust or singularly culpable in the crucifixion of Jesus. And who could blame them? Two white crosses marked the spot on the highway where the accident occurred. Yet throughout his ordeal David reminded me of myself; of my own sin and moral culpability. He was not alone in his need. There was a glaring obviousness about his evil, but it did not obscure my own.

David honestly grieved over what he had done, which is very different from feeling pity for what he had become. He tried to understand his actions but he did not excuse them. He was filled with remorse and repentance. Did Jesus have David in mind when he prayed, "Father, forgive them for they know not what they do?" Yes, indeed. Whether there is an empty six-pack in the trunk or some leftover crucifixion spikes in our pockets, we all need to repent and turn to Christ for forgiveness. We all need Jesus to pray for us, "Father, forgive them for they do not know what they are doing."

Reflections on the Way

Why was Jesus silent before his accusers?

What is the significance of his prayers from the cross?

How does Jesus' prayer from the cross prove that no one is beyond the scope of God's mercy?

If Jesus prayed this way, how should we pray?

"My God, My God"

"From noon until three in the afternoon darkness came over all the land. About three in the afternoon Jesus cried out in a loud voice, 'Eli, Eli, lema sabachthani?' (which means 'My God, my God, why have you forsaken me?')." Matthew 27:45-46

Of all Jesus' words from the cross this is the hardest one to hear. As Spurgeon said, "it is measureless, unfathomable, inconceivable. The anguish of the Savior on your behalf and mine is no more to be measured and weighed than the sin which needed it, or the love which endureth it."[1] The first three sayings from the cross show Christ's love for others: Jesus prayed for his enemies ("Father, forgive them for they know not what they do"), he promised salvation to the repentant thief ("Today, you will be with me in paradise"), and he showed his affection for Mary ("Woman, behold your son"). Everyone near the cross was prayed for and ministered to. At the cross Jesus declared *forgiveness*, *salvation* and *affection*. However, in his fourth statement, Jesus cried out to God in a loud voice, "My God, my God, why have you forsaken me?" Jesus' ministry has been marked by an absolute oneness with the Father, but in this anguished prayer we count the terrible price Jesus paid to free us from the power of sin and death.

The very essence of Jesus' ministry was his fellowship with the Father. Everything he did reflected his immediate and intimate fellowship with the Father. Jesus knew from the outset that he was

1. Spurgeon, *Christ's Words from the Cross*, 51.

headed to the cross and he knew why. "For even the Son of Man did not come to be served, but to serve, and to give his life as a ransom for many" (Mark 10:45). On several occasions he explained to his disciples "that he must go to Jerusalem and suffer many things . . . and that he must be killed and on the third day be raised to life" (Matt 16:21). The explanation he would later give to the disciples on their way to Emmaus was in his mind from the beginning: "Did not the Christ have to suffer these things and then enter his glory?" (Luke 24:26). We are taken aback by his reasoning that claims his fellowship with the Father is tied into his obedient sacrifice on our behalf. "The reason my Father loves me is that I lay down my life— only to take it up again" (John 10:17).

"Our faith fails us, and then we think that God has forsaken us," wrote Spurgeon, "but our Lord's faith did not for a moment falter, for He says twice, 'My God, my God.' Oh, the mighty double grip of His unhesitating faith! He seems to say, 'Even if Thou hast forsaken Me, I have not forsaken Thee.'"[2] Herein lies the greatest paradox of all time. The one in whom fellowship with the Father was his right by virtue of his being, and the one in whom fellowship with the Father was his right by virtue of his faithfulness and obedience, was completely forsaken and totally abandoned by the Father because of us. Instead of being honored, he was condemned; instead of being praised, he was accused. "Yet it was the Lord's will to crush him" (Isa 53:10).

Jesus' cry from the cross embraces and comprehends all the lamentations of all God's people throughout all of time. All other cries of anguish, all other "Gethsemanes," all other "Golgothas," look to this moment for resolution. It is as if Jesus literally gathered up all the lamentations of God's people and shouted them from the cross in a loud voice. This includes Abraham's unspoken anguish on Mount Moriah and Job's passionate lament from the ash heap and David's utter feeling of God-forsakenness.

But no one had ever uttered this cry the way Jesus did. For Abraham, Job, and David, the absence of God *seemed* very real, but for Jesus it was absolutely real. No one ever experienced the

2. Ibid., 53.

149

fellowship of the Father the way Jesus did, and no one experienced the burden and judgment of humanity's depravity the way Jesus did. Jesus' agony of soul was ultimately and most intensely spiritual. "Grief of mind is harder to bear than pain of body . . . Spiritual sorrows are the worst of mental miseries . . . .We can bear a bleeding body, and even a wounded spirit, but a soul conscious of desertion by God is beyond conception unendurable."[3]

In the crisis of Gethsemane and in the pain of the cross, Jesus anticipated and experienced the wrath of God. He deliberately identified with our sin and our alienation from God. "God made him who had no sin to be sin for us, so that in him we might become the righteousness of God" (2 Cor 5:21). "He was delivered over to death for our sins and was raised to life for our justification" (Rom 4:25). "He himself bore our sins in his body on the tree so that we might die to sins and live for righteousness, by his wounds you have been healed"(1 Pet 2:24). The intensity of his struggle came not from a fear of death, but from his real experience of God-forsakenness. "This marks the lowest depth of the Savior's grief. The desertion was real. . . . It was no delirium of mind, caused by weakness of body, the depression of his spirit, or the near approach of death. His mind was clear to the last. He bore up under pain, loss of blood, scorn, thirst, and desolation . . . .All the tortures on His body He endured in silence; but when it came to being forsaken by God, then His great heart burst out. . . . It was a real absence he mourned."[4]

Make no mistake about it, Jesus was truly abandoned by the Father, and having lived in the closest possible fellowship with the Father he knew in the depths of his being the significance of this terrible abandonment. The bystanders may have thought they heard Jesus say "Eli" instead of "Eloi" in any case they thought that Jesus was calling out for Elijah, "Listen, he's calling Elijah." Someone stuck a sponge soaked in wine vinegar on a pole and poked it in Jesus' face. The crowd mockingly said, "Let's see if Elijah comes to take him down." The solemn reverence reserved for

3. Ibid.
4. Ibid., 53-54.

the traditional celebration of the Passover lamb was replaced by mocking derision in the sacrifice of Christ, our Passover lamb.

One bystander did not go along with the crowd. The Roman centurion, "who stood there in front of Jesus" and "heard his cry and saw how he died," was unexpectedly changed by the whole experience. He praised God and said, "Surely this was a righteous man" (Luke 23:47). Mark described the centurion's testimony more dramatically, "Surely this man was the Son of God!" There is no naturalistic explanation for this confession. How does one go from witnessing Jesus' death on a cross to confessing that he is the Savior of the world? From a human point of view, we are much more likely to join in mocking derision than to bow in worship. The startling truth is that at that very moment when Jesus hung dying on the cross, when our Savior not only felt God-forsaken, but was, in fact, God-forsaken because of our sin, the Father was revealing and convicting the Roman centurion in charge of the crucifixion of the true identity of Jesus.

Spurgeon was right when he said, "You shall measure the height of His love, if it be ever measured, by the depth of His grief, if that can ever be known."[5] We cannot fathom either the depths of Jesus' despair nor the limits of His love, but we can respond to him in love and obedience.

Reflections on the Way

How can we take comfort from Jesus' cry from the cross?

What did God-forsaken abandonment mean to Jesus?

To what extent did Jesus identify with us in our sin?

How do you explain the Roman Centurion's testimony at the cross?

5. Ibid., 52.

"Father!"

"Jesus called out with a loud voice, 'Father, into your hands I commit my spirit.' When he said this, he breathed his last." Luke 23:46

Jesus ends his earthly ministry with a shout. His final prayer testifies to his complete control. "I lay down my life—only to take it up again. No one takes it from me, but I lay it down of my own accord. I have authority to lay it down and authority to take it up again. This command I received from my Father" (John 10:17-18). The power of the resurrection lies behind each of Jesus' statements from the cross, but especially this final prayer. If the bones of Jesus Christ disintegrated in a Palestinian tomb then there is no forgiveness, no offer of salvation, no comfort in the midst of sorrow, no resolution of spiritual anguish, no provision for pain, and no redemption for the soul. If Christ has not been raised from the dead, we have only a Buddhist lesson in suffering, an Islamic example of martyrdom, a Jewish act of nonconformist zeal, and a humanist illustration of fate. The Apostle Paul said it bluntly, "If Christ has not been raised, our preaching is useless and so is your faith" (1 Cor 15:14).

Jesus died on Friday, but by Sunday he was explaining why "the Messiah had to suffer these things and then enter his glory" to two discouraged disciples heading home to Emmaus (Luke 24:26). They didn't recognize him. They were depressed; "downcast" is the word Luke used. They were discussing Jesus in the past tense. "He *was* a prophet," they lamented, "powerful in word and deed before

God and all the people. The chief priests and our rulers handed him over to be sentenced to death, and they crucified him; but we had hoped that he was the one who was going to redeem Israel." They were also bewildered. Before leaving Jerusalem they heard reports that the tomb was empty. "Some of our women amazed us," they said. "They came and told us that they had seen a vision of angels, who said he was alive!" Discouraged and confused, they were unaware that they were in the presence of the risen Lord. "How foolish you are," Jesus declared, "and how slow of heart to believe all that the prophets have spoken! Did not Christ have to suffer these things and then enter his glory?" "And beginning with Moses and all the Prophets, he explained to them what was said in all the Scriptures concerning himself" (Luke 24:27).

The truly surprising fact is that Jesus expected to find believers, not skeptics or cynics. He offered them no sympathy for their confusion; no solace for their downcast spirits. "How foolish you are, and how slow of heart to believe . . ." Jesus didn't "knock their socks" off with a celestial sermon. He simply recounted the facts, discussed the truths, and explained the Scriptures. When they finally did recognize Jesus, it was the conversation that inspired them. "Were not our hearts burning within us while he talked with us on the road and opened the Scriptures to us?"

In the end, Jesus on the cross is either a picture of human fate without hope or he is the atoning sacrifice that we accept by faith. We cannot be persuaded or convinced of the meaning of Jesus' cross or the reality of his resurrection apart from work of God. What Jesus did for those two disciples, he desires to do for us. Through the Holy Spirit he seeks to bring us to faith and trust in him. As the Apostle Paul said, "Our message is not with wise and persuasive words, but with a demonstration of the Spirit's power, so that your faith might not rest on human wisdom, but on God's power." Paul added, "We have not received the spirit of the world but the Spirit who is from God, that we may understand what God has freely given us" (1 Cor 2:4-5,12).

The final word from the cross was a shout not a gasp, a declaration of hope, not a cry of despair. Instead of giving up,

Jesus offered up; instead of surrendering to fate, he committed himself in faith. Not a note of resignation, but the expectation of resurrection. Not a sigh of relief, but a prayer of confidence. The God who prays invites us to join him in prayer. Even though this prayer was uniquely his own, Jesus meant for us to pray as he had prayed, "Father, into your hands I commit my spirit." The first Christian martyr, Stephen, followed the example of Jesus. "While they were stoning him, Stephen prayed, 'Lord Jesus, receive my spirit'" (Acts 7:59).

Into whose hands will you give your life? Only the one true and living God, Father, Son, and Spirit is worthy of your belief and mine. He alone is able to guard what we have entrusted to his care (2 Tim 1:12). This is not a prayer to be prayed only at the end of life, but a prayer to be prayed today. As Jesus gave himself into the Father's hands, so we give ourselves into the hands of God. Today is the day to pray, "Father, into your hands I commit my spirit."

Reflections on the Way

How is the God who prays teaching us how to pray?

Why is Jesus' life so much more than a great example to us?

We have described Jesus as the God who kneels, the God who comforts, and the God who prays. Why does he becomes our best guide to living the Christian life?

Why should Jesus' final prayer from the cross be our daily prayer?

Bibliography

Aalen, S. "Glory." In *Dictionary of New Testament Theology*, edited by Colin Brown, vol.2, 44-45. Grand Rapids: Zondervan, 1976.

Anderson, Ray S. *Historical Transcendence and the Reality of God: A Christological Critique*. Grand Rapids: Eerdmans, 1975.

Augustine. *Homilies on the Gospel of John: Nicene and Post-Nicene Fathers*. Vol. 7, first series. Edited by Philip Schaff. Peabody, MA: Hendrickson, 1995.

Barclay, William. *The Gospel of John, vols. 1-2*. Philadelphia: Westminster, 1975.

Barth, Karl. *Dogmatics in Outline*. New York: Harper, 1959.

Barth, Markus. *Ephesians: The Anchor Bible*. Vol. 34. New York: Doubleday, 1974.

Beasley-Murray, George R. *John: Word Biblical Commentary*. Vol. 36. Waco, TX: Word, 1987.

Brown, Raymond E. *The Gospel According to John: The Anchor Bible*. Vols. 29 & 29A. New York: Doubleday, 1970.

Bruner, Frederick Dale. *The Churchbook: Matthew*. 2 vols. Grand Rapids: Eerdmans, 2004.

————. *The Gospel of John: A Commentary*. Grand Rapids: Eerdmans, 2012.

Bruce, F. F. *The Epistle to the Hebrews*. Grand Rapids: Eerdmans, 1990.

Carson, D. A. *The Gospel According to John*. Grand Rapids: Eerdmans, 1991.

Casper, Jayson, and Tom Osanjo. "When Christians Say the Shahada." *Christianity Today*, July/August 2015, 20-21.

Chamber, Oswald. *My Utmost For His Highest: The Updated Edition in Today's Language*. Edited by James Reimann. Grand Rapids: Discovery House, 1992.

Chrysostom, John. "Homilies on the Gospel of John: LXXXI and LXXXII." In *Nicene And Post-Nicene Fathers*, vol. 14, first series, edited by Philip Schaff, 299-306. Peabody, MA: Hendrickson, 1995.

Cockerill, Gareth Lee. *The Epistle To The Hebrews*. Grand Rapids: Eerdmans, 2012.

France, R. T. *Matthew: The Tyndale New Testament Commentaries*. Grand Rapids: Eerdmans, 1985.

Greidanus, Sidney. *Preaching Christ from the Old Testament: A Contemporary Hermeneutical Method*. Grand Rapids: Eerdmans, 1999.

Harvey, Thomas Alan. *Acquainted with Grief: Wang Mingdao's Stand for the Persecuted Church in China*. Grand Rapids: Brazos, 2002.

Horton, Michael S. "How the Kingdom Comes." *Christianity Today* 50/1 (January 2006) 42–46.

Hunter, James Davison. *To Change the World: The Irony, Tragedy, & Possibility of Christianity in the Late Modern World*. New York: Oxford University Press, 2010.

Kapolyo, Joe. "Matthew." In *Africa Bible Commentary*, edited by Tokunboh Adeyemo, 1105–70. Grand Rapids: Zondervan, 2006.

Kennedy, Rick. *The First American Evangelical: A Short Life of Cotton Mather*. Grand Rapids: Eerdmans, 2015.

Kierkegaard, Søren. *Attack Upon 'Christendom.'* Translated by Walter Lowrie. Princeton, NJ: Princeton University Press, 1968.

———. *Purity of Heart Is To Will One Thing*. New York: Harper & Row, 1956.

———. *Training in Christianity*. Translated by Walter Lowrie. Princeton, NJ: Princeton University Press, 1957.

Lewis, C. S. *Mere Christianity*. New York: Collier, 1960.

———. *The Problem of Pain*. New York: Collier, 1962.

———. *The Screwtape Letters*. New York: Harper One, 2001.

———. *The Weight of Glory*. New York: Collier, 1962.

Luther, Martin. *The Complete Sermons of Martin Luther*. Vol. 5. Edited by Eugene F. A. Klug. Grand Rapids: Baker, 2000.

Malone, Andrew S. "God The Illeist: Third-Person Self-References And Trinitarian Hints in the Old Testament." *JETS* 52/3 (September 2009) 499–518.

Morris, Leon. *The Gospel According to John*. Grand Rapids: Eerdmans, 1971.

McCarthy, Cormac. *The Sunset Limited*. New York: Vintage, 2006.

McKnight, Scot. *1 Peter: The NIV Application Commentary*. Grand Rapids: Zondervan, 1996.

Newbigin, Lesslie. *The Light Has Come: An Exposition of the Fourth Gospel*. Grand Rapids: Eerdmans, 1982.

Origen. *Origen: An Exhortation to Martyrdom, Prayer and Selected Works*. The Classics of Western Spirituality. Edited by R. Greer. New York: Paulist, 1979.

Packer, J. I. *Knowing God*. Downers Grove, IL: InterVarsity, 1973.

Ross, Allen P. *Recalling the Hope of Glory*. Grand Rapids: Kregel, 2006.

Spurgeon, Charles H. *Christ's Words from the Cross*. Grand Rapids: Baker, 1997.

Temple, William. *Readings in St. John's Gospel*. London: Macmillan, 1959.

Tennent, Timothy. "Gospel Clarity vs. 'The Fog'" posted Tuesday, December 16, 2014 at www.timothytennent.com.

Thielicke, Helmut. *The Evangelical Faith*. 3 vols. Grand Rapids: Eerdmans, 1977.

Webster, Douglas D. *The God Who Kneels*. Eugene, OR: Cascade Books, 2015.

White, R. E. O. *Christian Ethics*. Philadelphia: John Knox, 1981.

———. "Salvation." In *Evangelical Dictionary of Theology*, edited by Walter A. Elwell, 967–69. Grand Rapids: Baker, 1984.